SUPERBIKING

SUPERBIKING

Blackett Ditchburn

Photography by Don Morley

Published in 1983 by Osprey Publishing Limited
27A Floral Street, London WC2E 9DP
Member company of the George Philip Group
First reprint autumn 1984
Second reprint winter 1985
Third reprint spring 1986

British Library Cataloguing in Publication Data
Ditchburn, Blackett
    Superbiking.
    1. Motorcycling
    I. Title
    796.7   GV1059.5
ISBN 0-85045-487-5

Editor Tim Parker

Filmset and printed in England by
BAS Printers Limited, Over Wallop, Hampshire

*The publisher insists that personal safety is solely the
responsibility of the motorcycle rider and that they will not
accept liability—in connection with this publication—for
any accident, injury, or damage to either vehicles, person
or persons.*

Contents

1 So you think you can ride?

Motorcycles are all about excitement. Once perhaps, they were considered a sensible, economical form of personal transport, if a little downmarket. But things have changed. In the rush to woo the customer with faster and more impressive machines, manufacturers have unwittingly or even deliberately made the decision to buy and ride a motorcycle an emotional one. The thrill of it all reigns supreme above all else.

So the individual who seeks to kick mediocrity in the face and find excitement chooses a fast motorcycle as the vehicle for self expression. Who can resist the headlong rush of acceleration from a superbike, the satisfaction of taking a particular corner faster than ever before or the sensitivity needed to brake hard, front tyre squirming for grip. All along knowing that you, alone in the world, are responsible for every element of stability. That without you, this whole set-up would turn into an out of control lump of metal unable even to remain upright.

This book is dedicated to anyone who understands those first two paragraphs. To anyone who is not afraid to admit to the thrill of riding fast and well and moreover, to those who wish to explore the absolute limits, look over the edge and yet return safely to tell the tale.

Today's motorcycle is a sophisticated machine, far removed from its ancestors. It is not hard to see the difference since development has produced a machine superior in almost every respect. But the development has been totally technological. How much time has been spent teaching improved riding ability? Let's not confuse riding ability with road safety either. Follow to the letter the edicts of the road safety buffs and you will indeed ride safely, but you certainly won't find riding a motorcycle very exciting. So on the one hand, the whole of motorcycling is dedicated to excitement. Motorcycle manufacturers sell their machines by publicising them as more exciting than ever before. Vast catalogues of accessories are available to make your chosen machine even quicker and more exciting. It is undeniable that the majority of motorcyclists ride to find excitement.

Yet on the other hand, every training scheme for the road rider tends to take up a wholly contrary attitude. In a strange way most training organisations seem to deny the existence of the excitement demon and thus deny the most important motivating factor in motorcycling. Nevertheless, official training is desirable, even if it appears to be stodgy apart, of course, from the legal necessity in some countries. In the following pages we are going to examine riding techniques without taking away the thrills, maybe introduce a few more thrills and with luck, enable the rider to gain more from his machine in every way. All in safety.

Take a large fistful of one hundred brake horsepower and you will realise that superbikes demand ready and aware riders. Not merely to tame the awesome power but to get the most from the machine, to take it as fast

How did you learn to ride?

as it will go without ever letting the machine take over. Most superbike owners are responsible enough to be aware of their own limitations but at the same time most will find that they can still learn about riding techniques which help to push back their own frontiers of ability. The greater the appreciation, so will the satisfaction be greater.

With cornering in particular too many are riding in the unknown surviving purely on subconscious, animal ability. In reality, every aspect of a cornering machine can be analysed, learned and consequently improved. Take each part of riding a motorcycle, examine it in this way and the result will be immense satisfaction from conquering the motorcycle—of always being in control while rushing to personal and mechanical limits.

This is not, however, a doctrine dedicated to highway lunacy. Throughout this book I will be breaking a few popular misconceptions and advocating a new approach to motor-

The open road beckons

cycling. But I am working from a positive standpoint hoping to improve, for everyone's benefit, the entertainment value of two wheels. With motorbike technology developing so rapidly it's time to re-appraise the weakest link in the chain—the skills of riding. These are skills which can be taught and just like any other activity some people will display a natural ability which distinguishes them from the rest.

There is too great a gulf between those with devil-may-care natural flair and those who learn by their mistakes. In the whole ancestry of motorcycle training there has not been an attempt either to channel natural ability onto an improved level or to lift average skills and aptitude onto an altogether higher plane. So far, books about riding have been safety conscious, rewritten versions of the Highway Code or police manual and have rarely even included discussion on the process of actually riding and controlling the bike. Riders are left to their own devices when it comes to discovering the capabilities of themselves and their bike.

Bearing this in mind, Government policy and burgeoning legislation will not remove the root cause of the accident statistics it so worries about but will merely harangue riders with a series of rules and recommendations which remain partially effective, if at all.

With this book examining performance and speed, it would be easy to feel that you have to be in possession of the latest superbike before any of it begins to apply. This is not true—it applies to any powered two wheel vehicle in some part. Except in extreme circumstances, power and weight does not effect the steering principle. Mopeds and superbikes track through bends in the same manner.

Riding safely in company needs a different approach

Spirited riding need not be dangerous

It seems that modern technology is pushing towards more compact machines with a performance hitherto associated with weighty superbikes. Light weight, high power and quick, accurate steering make for a very demanding motorcycle. So it is ever more pressing that the rider is better qualified for the task in front of him. The swifter and surer you progress on such quick and responsive machinery, how much greater the satisfaction. When you are in control of every human input, how much greater the rewards.

Our roads are becoming more and more congested. That is the price we pay for the progress of our civilisation. It also elevates the motorcyclist to the privileged position of the last of the road users to be able to make unhindered progress, to enjoy the road and its relationship to his machine as much as the passing scenery. It also puts him in a dangerous position. Breaking free from the nose-to-tail drudgery is fine but it means that more often than not a motorcyclist will be passing other vehicles.

Overtaking is visibly one of the most hazardous manoeuvres any road user makes. The motorcyclist on board his inherently unstable machine, far more exposed than his four wheeled counterpart, has to balance the safety odds in his favour if he is to make confident progress. Tipping that balance is easier for a rider who knows what he is doing.

Riding well comes from within. Only you, holding the handlebars, feeling the road through the tyres and suspension, can really tell how consistent and safe is your progress. In isolated conditions, such as on a racetrack, it is possible for observers to give helpful comment on how to improve technique. Most riders, for most of the time, do not have a valued second opinion. They have to be self taught.

Unfortunately, riders find themselves in a difficult situation. As I have said, riding a motorcycle can be taught. Just like any other skill, however, you need to reach a fairly high level of competence before really appreciating what you have been taught.

The motorcyclist faces the challenge of reaching this point safely. So far it has been left to the individual to find his way there. Too many have, perhaps literally, fallen by the wayside without ever discovering the real satisfaction motorcycling can offer.

Sporting bikes need ready riders

Playing around is fun too, but away from others

If this book is successful, I hope it will help a few riders to make safer progress towards putting together that intangible collection of skills that make riding safely and fast such a joy.

Along the way I hope to smash a few myths that have built up around motorcycling. The mystique that surrounds handling and steering and the real abilities of bike and rider must be blown away if we are really to raise our riding standards. If you already ride well then you are already a victim of that mystique. Even the fastest men in the world—grand prix riders—admit that they are constantly learning about the high speed mix of man and machine.

Motorbikes, ridden properly, are the most manoeuverable machines on the road. They accelerate faster than cars. They stop better than cars. They are slimmer, lighter and can change direction quicker than cars. This may seem like stating the obvious but always remember that a car remains in a stable condition almost irrespective of what the driver does. The stable condition of a motorcycle is totally the responsibility of the rider.

What more of an excuse do you need to go out riding more often if any basic riding ability can be improved with practice?

2 Riding in style—not sliding down the road

Before you leap out of the front door and disappear at wheelie popping speed in a haze of smoking tyres for the first peg-scraping, knee-dragging corner you can find . . . pause for thought. Your enthusiasm for bikes has developed far enough for you to be reading this book so don't blow it by being stupid. Broken bones may be a badge of courage to some but they do stop you from being out there riding. Stuck in bed or hobbling with a stick, talking about what you are going to do is not the same as actually doing it.

Yes, you have heard it all before but you simply cannot escape the fact that motorcycles are dangerous. That's probably why they are so exciting, but ride with brains and you can make rapid progress in complete safety. Motorbikes will have become less dangerous.

Throughout this book I am going to be looking at advanced techniques, often ones that only a few motorcyclists have ever really appreciated. If you don't treat such techniques with a healthy respect and a cautious approach—watch out—for you will never find out just what riding is all about.

It's up to you and no-one else to take a sensible approach to your riding. Unfortunately, the consequences of irresponsibility are not necessarily confined to the rider. As an example, when I was just beginning my motorcycling the following story was reported in the local newspaper.

It seems that a guy was out on his bike—the then highly desirable Kawasaki Hl 500—one Sunday afternoon. It was sunny that afternoon, I had been out on my own bike as well. I know how he must have felt, riding down dry, tree lined roads with the sunshine dappling down. I can see, too, why he began to hurry along, enjoying the speed and acceleration of his bike.

Why did he decide to overtake just before the brow of a hill? With an estimated impact speed of 130 mph he hit a bus coming the other way head on. His mate, riding pillion behind—totally incapable of doing anything to stop such insane riding, powerless to control his own destiny—died as well. What was the point?

He didn't lose control of his bike, just his excitement. So there is the first and absolutely the most important rule in motorcycling—never do anything over which you do not have full control and can safely predict the outcome.

Many riders with a few years experience seem to find this golden rule naturally and as a result they are safe, secure riders. That is why insurance rates come tumbling down as you get older. At the same time, however, experience for many of these riders equates with vast safety margins. They cease to hustle corners to any great degree, since cranking it over still preserves the fear of the unknown. They are no longer exploring the capabilities of themselves or their machine.

The fun of motorcycling lies in never stopping learning, never switching onto autopilot. Satisfaction comes from blending concentration with excitement.

15

Danger lurks everywhere

Take a gentle approach to the following chapters, experimenting with new techniques sensibly. Find quiet, open roads or deserted car parks on which to experiment and develop new skills. Approach everything as gently as possible but forcefully enough to understand the full effect. It is a delicate balance to strike and since only the rider can appreciate the feedback from the machine, it is his responsibility to take a cautious approach and preserve safety.

You don't become a world champion overnight, so don't expect to read this book once and end up the perfect rider. Use it as a handbook, constantly referring back to check your observations with those predicted. Unless you are already a skilled mechanic you would never dream of doing a complete engine rebuild without a workshop manual. It makes life so much easier. Treat this book as your riding workshop manual.

It may prove difficult for some but if you are going to draw any real, tangible benefit, you will have to be particularly humble and

The effects of speed must not be underestimated

Never let excitement get the upper hand

honest with yourself. There is no point in saying, 'Right, I can do that perfectly, now what?' If you are really honest, only in the rarest cases will you do something perfectly. Absolute honesty is required at every stage if you really want to predict personal limits. Often, racers are heard to comment that they were racing 'on the limit.' Only by being very critical of their own ability have they been able to ride on the limit and not go over it. Be hum-ble enough to recognise if some aspect of your riding is wrong or inadequate and take sensible steps to correct the fault.

Always remember that every motorcyclist, just like an athlete, has both physical and mental limits which no amount of practice will push back. Take any motorcyclist. Just like the sprinter, he can run a hundred metres—but nowhere near as fast. If the motorcyclist trains hard, gets himself fit and

Concentrate on staying alive

Spare a thought for the passenger

studies running technique, he will get faster and may even begin to challenge the athlete in terms of speed. This will not happen overnight and the same applies to riding. Accept that somewhere within you there is an absolute limit to your abilities. With the aid of the few guidelines set out in this book you are going to work towards those limits. Apply sufficient sense and you won't exceed them.

The danger element in motorcycling will often interfere with this process, setting up false barriers which, although a rider may believe to be his absolute limits, are really very easily exceeded by relaxing a little and thinking about what is happening.

Once again, be warned that speed crazed lunatics have no place on the highway, least of all aboard a motorcycle. As anyone with track experience will tell you, neither do they have a place on a racetrack. Irresponsibility is not praised by anyone. So don't bother trying if you cannot contain yourself.

Street riding takes place in an uncontrolled environment where many things totally beyond the control of the rider can happen to affect safe progress. Road surfaces can change; there may be mud or oil just around the next bend; other vehicles can pull out in front of you and stop unexpectedly. Manhole covers, bumps and potholes just add to the whole mixture of unpredictability. A good road rider must learn to expect these problems and be prepared to cope either by taking avoiding action or by developing the ability to ride through or over the obstruction. As mentioned, these problems can happen at any time and anywhere. The motorcyclist must be in full control all the time in order to take safe, quick and appropriate action whenever necessary. Greater awareness and better control lessen the dangers of road riding but nothing will eliminate them completely.

Beyond all this doom, gloom and boring warning there is a real and valid point. True safety consciousness, born of confidence and knowledge makes riding more enjoyable. This 'sixth sense' helps you to relax and enjoy the ride, unfettered by misplaced, nervous worrying. Good and practised anticipation will lessen the number of emergency situations demanding hurried reaction. Often, the rider with a studied and sensible style will travel considerably faster and definitely with less risk than the insensitive, over excited street racer.

There is a limit, too, as to just how much can be experienced on the roads where so many other factors contribute to the dangers. A controlled environment is the only place to experience the real extremes of motorcycling. Take to the race track to find out just how far over a motorbike can lean. Racing schools are an ideal way of doing this without too much expense.

By removing most of the unpredictability found on the highway, racing schools provide a distilled excitement. The process is a humbling one. Shown the unending strip of racetrack most riders will feel the adrenalin surge. Once out on the circuit, especially for the first time, the unbelievable speed of professional racers is brought home. You discover that corners take on a new meaning. That somehow, all that dramatic, dashing technique you have spent hours rehearsing on backstreets and country lanes is hopelessly inadequate.

Experiment gently

If you are fearless enough, after a few laps the handlebars will seem to be about to touch the ground on slow bends and on the faster ones, you will begin to think the tyres are made of glue. If you are skilled (and lucky) enough, you won't fall off. When you get off and the sheer excitement has died down, sit back and realise just how much has been learnt. An experience like this will totally readjust your approach to riding.

Unfortunately, learning on a track is a far cry from riding on the public road. Remember the unpredictability of the highway environment, the fact that other people cannot be relied on. Frustrating though it is, the trained, good rider will hardly ever be able to stretch his abilities on public roads. This, however, is the standard for which we all must try. Because once you know where your personal limits are, then preserving a sensible safety margin can be more precise.

If the racetrack gives as near to complete predictability in terms of surface as you could wish for, the trail park or off-road track provides the complete opposite. They, too, are unparalleled good fun. At first consideration, it may seem that tearing around a muddy arena of bumps, jumps and ferocious U-turns has little opportunity for the road rider to improve his skills. Nothing could be further from the truth.

Off-road, everything happens to the extreme and hardly ever at excessively dangerous speed. You find out how an off-road bike will slide under braking and acceleration; how bikes feel as if they lose weight over bumps, even lose contact with the ground; how quick your reactions are when things start to go wrong. Above all, you become aware that motorcycles move independently of the rider—the two are not a fixed unit. In normal road conditions the bike and rider may feel like a unit when twitching or wobbling due to some outside influence. Many riders fail to appreciate that they can separate themselves from the machine by standing up or at least moving weight around on the footpegs. When riding off-road, normal steering can become a bit inadequate at times due to loose or slippery surfaces. When this happens you realise how important the transfer of bodyweight is to help steer a motorbike.

The value of off-road riding is considerable and you are usually in the happy position of being able to experiment on someone else's bike! Trail parks are great fun and if you think about what you are doing will teach you a great deal as well.

Somehow, somewhere, all the absolute extremes of motorcycle handling can be experienced often with the benefit of a qualified teacher. If you have the opportunity, use it.

This chapter has looked at the rider's approach to safety, usually one of the most important aspects to motorcycling. 'It will never happen to me' does not apply to motorcycling. Without a little bit of sense it is a racing certainty it will happen to you.

3 Scratcher's sensitivity

So just what has sensitivity to do with motor-cycling? When you're out there trying hard, street racing like the last of the scratchers, carving shiny marks into the hard steel of foot-pegs and exhausts, where does sensitivity come in? The truth is every single action, each single thought should be charged with nerves, searching and responding to every machine reaction and the developing road ahead.

Like everything else, sensitivity can be developed with practice and experience. When you rode your first bike, remember how all the controls felt alien? You would have been unable to tell whether the brakes were good, bad or plain indifferent. Yet now, perhaps after only a short period of experience, everything seems to come naturally. Often so much so that you forget entirely about the most basic functions of your bike. Clutch, gears, brakes and throttle are all just a means to an end and once mastered are never reconsidered. Think again.

In simple terms a motorcycle is a tool to take you from one place to another. It is a very complex tool but as with any other, the principles and techniques necessary to make it move with maximum efficiency must be studied and learned.

With the motorcycle both hands and both feet are fully occupied pulling, pressing and twisting the controls. Each one must receive the fullest attention. Even if you have been riding for years, think about the techniques for mastering each of the controls and as you read through the rest of this book see how they all come together to provide smooth, stylish riding.

Beginning with brakes, imagine you are sitting on your bike. You are cruising, relaxed and easy on a straightforward road. In the split second warning you of an emergency could you shut off the throttle completely, brake as hard as possible front and rear, both wheels close to the lock up point and change down for extra rear end control at the same time? In theory bikes can pull up in a shorter distance than any other vehicle. More often than not lack of rider awareness, ability and feel for the bike lengthens stopping distances. For the fragile motorcyclist heading towards an immovable object, that's bad news.

The full implications of braking will be dealt with in another chapter but here we can consider the action of fingers and toes on their respective levers.

Central to all motorcycling technique is the right hand. Not only does it have the twistgrip to control but also around 80 per cent of the stopping power. (Linked braking systems, of course, change this.) Which all leads to the right hand performing some pretty complicated tasks. Ideally, you should be able to use the throttle and brake independently so that you can twist the throttle to downshift while braking hard. To the novice this may seem a daunting task but practice will make it come right.

Of the two tasks facing the right hand, braking must be the most important. The braking action should always be totally unhindered,

Don't trap braking fingers behind the lever

either by the machine or the poor grasp of the rider. Think about your braking fingers. Which ones do you use? It may be so subconscious that you will actually have to go and sit on the bike to find out.

If brakes are in good order, average stopping will only ever require two fingers, whatever your machine. The best two to use are index and middle finger. This is because, when necessary, it is easier to bring up the third and exceptionally, little finger onto the lever. If, when using middle finger and third, something demanded extra braking then it would be awkward and distracting to pull the index finger out from behind an already well squeezed brake lever. If it needs practice to get into the habit of using the first two fingers then take things gently at first and do not be scared to revert to old habits in an emergency. Until you are naturally using the correct fingers for all your braking, it may take undue concentration or cause a lack of feel.

Watch the best road racers and moto-crossers—they all start braking with the index

Keep it smooth

finger and then add others depending on how hard they need to brake.

Once this technique is mastered, move on to controlling the throttle irrespective of what the braking fingers are doing. The thumb is important here, so wrap it around underneath the twist grip. Practise throttle control by resting the braking fingers on the lever and then accelerating and decelerating. Get the feel of things just sitting on the bike with the engine dead. Twisting action can be helped by wrapping third and little fingers around the other side of the twist grip.

Of course, when no braking is necessary nor anticipated, all fingers can be wrapped around the twist grip in a tight fist that says, 'Go for it!' Don't be prepared to go for it unless you are happy about your ability to get on the brakes quickly. Another tip about braking is to use the whole length of the lever. The further your pull is to the end of the lever, the more leverage you have and the less effort is required.

Moving on to the left hand, here the task is much easier and if you think hard, it often seems as though you are longing for the right hand to be able to work equally smoothly and efficiently. We cannot demand a complete change in motorcycle design, however, and anyway the existing arrangement can be made to work perfectly adequately.

Basically, the same applies to clutch fingers as to those on the brake. The fundamental difference is that clutches should demand only a light, consistent pressure compared with the increasing pressure required by the front brake. Clutch action will become a habit, always using the same two (or more) fingers. It is a good idea, however, to keep at least one of your fingers wrapped around the handle-

Set up the corner, then power through it

bar. This provides a firmer grip, essential to keep in touch with the steering.

Talking about hands, let's mention what both of them together feel, through the handlebars. Learning to steer, as we shall see later, is the most crucial of the various capabilities of a motorcycle rider. For the moment, practise riding by holding the bars sympathetically rather than having them clamped in a vice-like grip. Over bumps and road irregularities they will perhaps shake and wobble a little. Let them. Relax and become sensitive to what the motorcycle is telling you. Later chapters will explain what all the signals mean and how to interpret them.

Winter will change everything. Fingers can get cold and stiff and the onset of 'dead finger' comes far earlier. Dead finger, or to give it the technical title, Reynauld's Syndrome, is the result of prolonged exposure to vibration and cold. Fingers lose their feel and stiffen up. The colder the weather, the quicker the onset of the problem.

If fingers lose their feel, you cannot expect them to relay what is happening. Making things doubly dangerous, winter weather usually produces the riskiest road surfaces which demand maximum sensitivity. So the rule must be to take things gently in cold weather, regularly flexing and wriggling the fingertips to keep the blood moving.

The best way to keep hands warm is with mittens but these keep the fingers all together. If you do use mittens, you cannot expect the feel and control that comes from wearing gloves.

Feet are often wrapped in heavy and clumsy motorcycle boots but do not presume this dictates that their action must be clumsy. The braking foot, usually the right and occasionally the left, has a difficult task. The rear brake is important if you want to achieve maximum braking force, providing that extra 20 per cent which may mean the difference between a collision and a close shave. Rear brakes, unfortunately, are prone to a lack of feel and it takes a lot of practice and concentration before you can be confident that when used in conjunction with the front brake, the rear brake is making its maximum contribution.

The way to learn how to use the rear brake is simply with lots of practice. There is no sure way of teaching what to feel for since bikes differ so much. So just keep on practising.

The other foot has to deal with the gearchange. Here a bit of concentration will help prevent missed gears with their associated, unnecessary stresses to the engine and gearbox. Gearchanging in particular is very individual to different bikes. Some are quick and light, others are slow with a rather solid feeling. The real point is, you must decide what kind of gearbox your bike has and treat it accordingly. There is no point in trying to get racing changes from a cumbersome set of cogs—it will only mean more crashed gears and very likely an early trip to the repair shop. A consistent, sympathetic and yet positive action is called for.

Having run through the individual aspects of each control and its relationship to your hands and feet, we now move on to consider putting them all together in flowing unison. It is surprising just how many people remain clumsy with the process of making a motorcycle move and stop. Ragged gearchanging can provoke an unstable condition and even skidding. It will also impose a considerable stress on the gearbox and particularly the final drive. Careful and sensitive, but not necessarily slow, use prolongs the life of your motorcycle.

Beginning with the basics, start the engine with the gearbox in neutral, pull in the clutch,

Neat, tidy—and fast

Covering the rear brake

pop it into first gear, feed in the power as you release the clutch and you're off.

Big deal. You have done it a million times already. But concentrate on making it smooth, on not wasting revs without using the power. When do you change gear? Do you know exactly when to do so, or do you just change erratically?

Modern motorcycles are powerful machines and get more powerful as the revs increase. Only occasionally does the increase in power work in direct proportion to the increase in revs. This is the power band effect.

Two-stroke motorcycles exhibit the power band characteristic more than a four stroke, though all but the strongest four stroke will show the same effect to some degree. Go out and find a long, empty road. Select a middle gear, say third and slow down to the minimum number of revs the engine will pull without stalling. Now start to accelerate as hard as possible. You will feel the bike pulling at an ever increasing rate. At some point, usually at about 60–70 per cent of maximum revs, the power will come in much stronger and will be sustained to the red line, tailing off very quickly afterwards. That is the power band.

On some of the more racy two strokes this is quite a pronounced phenomenon. On four strokes it is often only barely discernible. Be aware of it because if you really want to get a move on, that's where the real power lies and keeping the engine spinning in this sector is the secret to going fast.

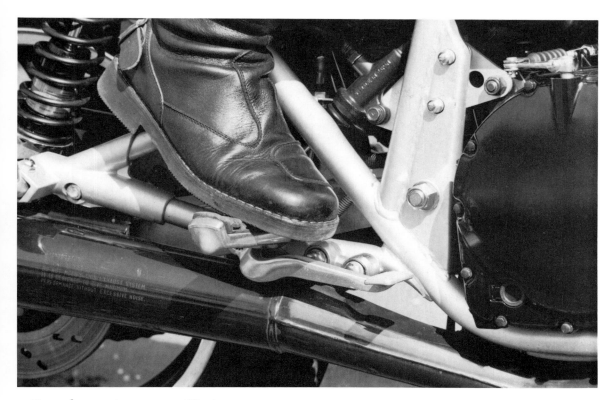

More comfortable and sensitive position

To make maximum use of first gear, a racer will pull away with the rev-counter needle firmly buried in the power band. Thus he is using maximum power to get his bike moving. In this situation, however, the clutch will become the throttle almost until top speed in first gear has been reached. It might sound odd but the rider, from a standing start, is maintaining maximum power and then slipping the clutch until gearbox and engine speed match rather than letting the clutch out as soon as possible at low revs and using the throttle to accelerate.

Present day clutches will take a lot of such hard use without showing too many ill effects, bringing to the road rider techniques which were once condemned as abuse or the province of racers only.

If you find you are in too high a gear, with the revs below the power band, there's a motocross technique which will get the revs up where they should be without having to change gear. It's called slapping the clutch and it means what it says. Keeping the throttle wide open, pull in the clutch and then let go. The engine will scream a bit and the bike will jump forwards, refreshed from a quick bite at the power that lurks at high revs. This technique could use a little care, though, particularly on the bigger bikes. It could give you a few hairy moments if tried halfway through a corner, too!

Slapping the clutch really only applies to the two stroke engine with a narrow power band. Larger bikes and four strokes usually generate sufficient torque outside the power band to make such methods redundant.

There are no hard and fast rules about when to change gear, so much depends on the bike and the road conditions. Primarily, however, the engine should never be allowed to snatch the transmission, the first sign that you are about to stall.

Be as consistent as you can. If you want to filter through traffic, rest the engine, perhaps changing up at only 40–50 per cent throttle. There is no point in changing out of first as soon as possible with the engine nearly stalling, then accelerating to screaming point in second only to slip quickly through third into fourth.

Once your engine is warm and you are off and moving, most modern gearboxes allow you to forget about the clutch and simply change gear by resting the throttle momentarily while shifting cogs. It's best to do this only for upward changes and return to the clutch for the downward ones.

Clutchless changes do not break any rules and done with care don't break any gearboxes either. While still accelerating, put gentle pressure on the gearshift to change up. The gearshift won't move, seemingly locked in place. The moment you throttle back, the gears will change, usually so quickly it will take some time to get used to. With a little practice, upward changes can become far faster and more effective. Drag racers have their own special version of this technique. Instead of throttling back, some use a thumb-operated ignition cut out so they can change gear without the need for fancy right hand operations.

It's best to reserve clutchless changes for brisk, unhindered acceleration and to take care in the lower gears. These usually have a wider spacing which can make it impossible to change smoothly except at very low revs.

Again, feel for the particular idiosyncrasies of your bike and allow for them, rather than try to force the bike to do something it was not designed for.

Changing down is a slightly more elaborate process and it is best always to use the clutch. Knocking it down a gear should really take place at around the same number of revs as changing up. If the conditions mean that you are changing up from third gear at 5000 rpm and this drops to 4000 rpm in fourth, then change back down again when the engine speed has fallen back to this level. This is a rough rule of thumb which gives a consistent, sensible ride. Never leave it in top until the last minute and then tap dance down to first. A motorcycle's engine braking lends stability to slowing down, so don't waste it.

On the down change, when the clutch is pulled in give the throttle a quick nudge—called blipping—just before letting the clutch out again. With practice, this will match the engine revs to the demands of the lower gear, avoiding any dangerous lurches and jerks. On bigger four strokes with vast amounts of engine braking, blipping the throttle is essential to avoid locking the back wheel every time you change down.

Much of this chapter has talked about engine speed in terms of revolutions per minute (rpm), illustrating the usefulness of a rev-counter. Most modern motorcycles have one and it's not just there for show. Use it.

Never coast with the clutch pulled in or the bike in neutral and make sure your bike is well maintained with the controls all adjusted properly. There's no point in developing great technique if cables are slack and brakes badly adjusted.

Dedicate yourself to breaking bad habits and keeping up your standards once you have achieved them. Concentrate on putting your use of all the controls into smooth harmony.

4 Grappling with gravity

One of the few skills nearly all aspiring motorcyclists possess is that of balance. From an early age they have probably ridden and played around on bicycles, developing the ability to keep two wheels upright.

So it's far too easy to overlook the basic balancing act, discounting the additional demands made by the greater weight and different steering geometry of a motorbike.

Average road riding takes place at speeds far removed from those employed weaving in and out of cones in the local school playground or municipal car park as practised by some training organisations. Superficially, many novices decry such manoeuvres as time wasting and tedious. But at least you can learn the rudiments of machine control at something less than lethal speeds. Every rider, however experienced, will benefit from developing an increased awareness of his balancing skills.

Just what is balance? What is the rider doing to keep the bike upright and moving in the direction he wants it to? Let's consider the instance of moving straight ahead quickly. As an example, try standing with one foot in front of the other in the same configuration as a motorcycle's wheels. Unless you were born and raised on a circus high-wire you will probably feel a bit wobbly. Your natural reaction will be to raise your arms and then move them around until you find a point of equilibrium. This is exactly what the rider is doing to keep his machine thundering onwards, aided by the gyroscopic reaction of the two wheels. He is keeping—balancing—identical weights either side of the line passing beneath the two wheels. When a corner arrives, things change completely but you will have to wait until the cornering chapter to find out how. For the moment we are only concerned with slow speed and straight line balancing, developing rider awareness of just what skills and reactions contribute to the bike's stability.

With the sensitivity analysed in the previous chapter, balance makes up the largest part of the stability that should be every rider's ideal. Once you know and understand what balance does to the machine then you will be better prepared to understand the reactions of bikes under braking, acceleration and particularly, cornering.

So basically, balance is keeping equal amounts of the combined weight of rider and machine on either side of the machine's centreline. Fine, how do we do that?

First and obvious step is to move your bodyweight about, since the motorcycle cannot move its weight from side to side of that centreline particularly easily. Or can it?

Try riding as slowly as possible in a straight line. Your natural reaction to prevent the machine from toppling over is to steer the bars from side to side. It works, too, seemingly catching each lurch before things fall with a clatter to the ground. To understand what you are doing to preserve this equilibrium, think a little about the geometry of the front fork of your motorcycle.

The fork pivots around the steering head,

Shuffle about to help tight turning

sloping forwards from that point. The actual fork legs are mounted in front of the frame headstock by triple clamps. Think about what this does to the contact patch of the front tyre when you are steering. It describes a small arc behind the steering axis, moving from side to side of the centreline in the straight ahead position.

Alternatively, you are moving the line between the two contact patches of front and rear tyres from side to side beneath the machine and hence redistributing the relative weight of machine either side of this line. Steering to the right puts more relative weight on the right hand side of the line and steering to the left, the opposite.

Which is all very well in theory and goes some way to explaining why a rider wobbles along at slow speed. Unfortunately, in practice there are too many other influences taking place for this to become very noticeable. Subconscious transfer of bodyweight will totally

Balance at speed is largely a natural reaction

confuse the issue and on larger machines, the friction generated by the front tyre will make steering at slow speed a brutish, indelicate action.

Let's go back to the straight line. By a combination of tweaking the steering and shifting bodyweight you are riding as slowly as possible. By the way, if you are aboard one of the larger machines you will also be using some pretty deft clutch control since most of these machines travel at running speed with their clutches engaged in first gear with the engine at tickover.

Often there is a temptation to allow your feet to hang down, soles skimming the road surface. It seems easier to ride this way, particularly in the earlier stages of learning. Remember standing with both feet in front of one another and using your arms to feel for balance? Since your hands are on the handlebars on a motorbike, or at least they should be, you cannot use your arms to search for balance. So dropping your feet and using your legs instead seems to be the answer. Whilst trailing legs and feet are a short term balancing aid it's a temptation that must be resisted in favour of the greater control that feet firmly on the pegs and a little practice will bring.

The main thing to learn is that the rider has infinite control over the centre of gravity between the two extremes of standing on the pegs and sitting on the machine with legs dangling. Experiment with your machine to see how these different extremes, and the positions in between, affect your riding ability.

To compromise without going to the extreme of standing up, move as far forward on the seat as possible, right up to the rear of the tank. This will give a greater degree of control over steering the handlebars left and right as they will be closer to you.

Move around to help cornering balance

Finding the real value of the hang-off style keeps lean to a minimum

This introduces the most important element in effective balancing—movement of the rider in relation to the machine. Too many people simply hop on and from then on consider themselves an immovable part of the bike. Scramble about. Move your bodyweight—usually about a quarter of the combined weight of man and machine—to the best position for easy balance and control.

When turning a tight circle at low speed for instance, let the bike lean down but counter-balance by sliding off the opposite side to the turn and moving forward for more control. It is really a case of using every technique available to help the balancing process. With larger superbikes, some with a very high centre of gravity, riding slowly calls for powerful, precise action. This action must be planned and

Allow the bike to tilt on tight turns but don't lean with it

considered because with all the extra weight and the grip of the front tyre, second chances are hard to come by.

Practising balance at slow speeds heightens awareness when things get a bit faster. Keep practising this slow control as often as possible—when filtering through traffic or rolling up to traffic lights. Skills like riding a motorcycle are largely learned by playing around trying out different attitudes and techniques. The more you learn at low speed about your

Body movement keeps things straight over high speed bumps

Bodyweight well off-centre gives optimum lean angle

machine, the better you will be able to predict its high speed behaviour. Playing around at high speed can have some disastrous consequences.

The faster you go, the less you seem to balance as the gyroscopic effect of the wheels begins to contribute and the machine seems to balance itself. The castor effect of the steering geometry helps this impression. The road surface is never perfectly smooth and every bump twitches the machine, theoretically throwing it off balance. These twitches are

... and back to descend

Trials techniques teach a lot

corrected subconsciously by the rider's innate sense of balance.

The handlebars become harder to move as the already mentioned castor effect of the front steering geometry takes over with increased speed. Wobbles, twitches and oscillations are damped out by the rider's arms, however, and moving weight around can still have a pronounced effect. Sliding back on the seat makes you more sensitive to the performance of a bike at high speed. You become more aware of the twitching, weaving and wobbling that goes on beneath you. Limitations of design mean wobbles of some kind are the case with

Stand up over large bumps. Lean forward to climb . . .

most bikes and equally, most of them keep such oscillations well under control. Sometimes though, things can get a little alarming as a particular weave develops into a regular yawing which is distinctly unsettling.

Modern motorcycle design is a compromise between high speed stability and low speed manoeuverability. So most production bikes steer well at relatively slow speeds and begin to get interesting, meaning more difficult, as speed increases. High speed twitchiness is provoked by many things, largely centred around the geometry of the bike, the tyres and the road surface.

Obviously it is impossible to make hard and fast rules about how to counteract these wobbles and weaves. These unsettling characteristics are the product of so many factors but broadly, lowering the centre of gravity will help to damp out wobbles.

Before an extreme situation occurs requiring such a drastic remedy as this, try moving your weight forwards on the machine. Usually, high speed wobbles can be attributed to the front end of the bike and hunching weight as far forward as possible is the answer. If a weave develops which threatens your control rather than standing up or any such acrobatics, lie flat on the tank, which will spread your weight forward and down. Either back off the throttle gradually or try to ride through it. If you pick the latter option, remember you will probably go back through the wobble as you slow down.

Keep a loose hold on the handlebars, too. With increasing wind resistance it is difficult to stop yourself acting as a wind break, attached to the handlebars by your arms. This means you are pulling hard on the handlebars and become insensitive to the small twitches which are so much a part of travelling quickly. Use your back and stomach muscles to lean forward into the wind, braced by a firm grip of the machine through your legs. Keep the touch on the handlebars light and you will often find the wobbles considerably eased. The earlier mentioned remedy for wobbles of lying on the tank takes the pull off the handlebars as well. No two motorcycles have the same weight balance or geometry, so expect considerable differences if you change machine. The whole learning process has to start again only next time you will have some guidelines on how to cope.

Some bikes are top heavy, others are well balanced but difficult to steer. Expect differences between machines but do not assume that one riding style will suit any bike. A style for one machine may not suit another but it can be great fun trying to find out what will work. Never make yourself uncomfortable trying to find a balance point. You will simply have less feel and probably mess something up if you are too contorted to use the controls properly. Never deliberately distract yourself from the real task in hand—riding safely.

A well developed sense of balance will help you to tell much earlier when the machine is about to become unstable or start to wobble. Quick detection and quick remedy help you to ride quicker and more confidently. The riding process then becomes one of fine tuning rather than wrestling.

5 The quick way to crash

Hauling on the brakes is usually the only way to avoid trouble. It can also be the quickest way to get you into trouble.

Those obvious and important facts are already established from earlier chapters and if you have read and understood chapter three you will now be searching for feel and response through your brake levers. Once this is achieved and the sensitivity of fingers and toes is as high as it can be, you have to consider how to use the brakes to maximum effect.

Most bikes have separate front and rear brakes and this unfortunately means that for the motorcycle's braking to be fully effective the rider needs sophisticated and sensitive techniques. Clumsy braking is the easiest way to end up throwing the whole bike down the road.

Wet weather makes slowing down a motorcycle an even more difficult task and not many can go through a whole riding career avoiding some kind of hairy moment through a combination of slippery roads and braking. So proceed with caution.

As we have said, the front brake provides around 80 per cent of the machine's braking capability. In the wet the grip of the front tyre lessens and trying to find an equivalent amount of stopping power will have the front wheel sliding every way except the direction in which you want it to go. Wet or slippy conditions must always be assessed individually as to what they can stand.

Whatever the conditions, always be prepared. Keep the reflexes practised and ready.

Which can often be easier said than done. Panic can have curious effects on otherwise normal people. Too frequently, motorcyclists take no evasive action at all in an emergency. With luck, and lots of it, you might get away with such tactics—but not often. Such panic induced inaction is a natural human reaction when faced with unexpected danger. So the answer is to always be prepared for the unexpected. Even when you are out on a gentle, unhurried ride keep searching for other vehicles pulling out in front of you, potholes in the road and all the other hazards that spell danger for the vulnerable motorcyclist. Imagine the complete unknown lurks everywhere. In this way, constantly aware of danger, you will anticipate the majority of emergencies and be prepared to take effective evasive action rather than doing nothing. You might be saving your life.

It is worth remembering that paralysis by panic is not the exclusive preserve of the motorcyclist—the motorist, cocooned in the safety of his car, is equally susceptible, if not more so. Do not expect others to take the evading action for you. Chances are they won't.

Thus braking, our greatest protector if used properly, can completely desert you when you need it most. At best a motorcycle will stop quicker than almost anything else on the road but this ideal situation will only occur with an experienced, skilful and above all aware rider.

Let's examine the braking process and assume that the roads are dry. On wet, slippy

Keep that back wheel on the ground

surfaces you simply should not be searching for absolute limits since they are far too unpredictable. On public roads the only thing to do in the wet is to ride to survive.

That said, from now on only practise braking technique on dry roads, always remembering the moving hazards of other road users.

Proficiency with the front brake is vital if you are to achieve maximum stopping power.

Braking in the top picture, accelerating in the bottom. Notice the difference in distance from front wheel to engine and change in available fork travel

You should already be using the correct fingers and through them trying to predict the slowing capacity of the front brake. One thing is certain. However hard you haul on the front brake, tyre scrabbling for grip and the suspension fully compressed, you are not going to launch yourself over the handlebars. Although it often feels as if the bike is going to wheelstand on the front end and spit you off, it won't. On some bikes this sensation is worse than on others but even with modern,

high traction tyres the greatest risk is for the front end to slide away from under you.

With the front brake forcing the machine nose-down, the rider's body is thrown forward with considerable force. In fact, modern bikes can generate nearly 0·9Gs of stopping power and this must be resisted by the rider.

When a motorcycle is braking hard, it tilts forward, forcing weight down through the contact patch of the front tyre on to the road. This in turn increases the tyre's grip and thus the braking capacity of the front wheel.

Although the front brake is crucial, bringing the rear into action cannot be

Braking into a corner. Check out the lack of front suspension

ignored. Braking hard will mean the rear brake will contribute the last few per cent of braking capacity. With forward transfer, the rear end becomes increasingly light and consequently the brake is sensitive and easier to lock up. A locked rear wheel is likely to step out of line and if the bike is cornering in the slightest, will be prone to slewing right around and spitting you off. A racer may often laugh like a maniac and dismiss the rear brake completely saying that if the rear wheel is on the ground you are not braking hard enough. Depending on the machine, rear wheels can indeed lift off the ground but a good rider will appreciate the benefits of keeping it in touch with terra firma and take all steps to make sure that it does. Once the back end is airborne the useful stabilizing effect of the rear wheel and brake is lost.

In hard braking, haul on the front brake first, followed a split second later by the rear. This gives a more predictable feel to the rear since most of the weight will already be thrown forwards by the time it is applied. If the rear brake is used first, when there is more weight bearing down through the back tyre, as the front brake is brought into action the rider will have to lessen his pressure on the rear brake to prevent the rear locking up.

How soon could you stop from this?

When the rear end does lock up the natural reaction is to release the brake to allow the tyre to regain grip and then re-apply for the extra stopping power. This, fortunately, is exactly the right technique but we must sound a note of caution. If the rear lock up occurs while cornering, releasing the brake to give rear wheel traction will cause it to hook up violently and throw you off over the high side. So straighten up as much as possible whenever the back end begins to slide, then take action as necessary. Better advice is not to let this wayward situation occur in the first place.

The second cautionary tale again revolves around your natural human instincts. If the back end locks up, as you release the pressure

to reapply, you will also subconsciously release some front brake pressure, further extending the already lengthened stopping distance. Avoiding this unfortunate state of affairs can only be done by making yourself aware of every single action taken and developing the skill necessary to use all the controls independently.

At the other end, front wheel lock up is frequently and wrongly talked about as the point of no return. Admittedly you need to be quicker witted to avoid disaster but momentary lock up can be quite controllable. With the extra weight of machine and rider thrusting down through the front tyre, impending lock up is easier to detect. As the breakaway point approaches, the bars will transmit a slightly rubbery feeling, almost as if they were about to snap sideways. This is about as much warning as you will get but is sufficient to give clear signals to the rider that he is as close to the limit as he dare go.

Although the front brake supplies some warning, don't be distracted if the rear breaks away while the front end alarm bells are ringing. Which provides all the more reason to be as skilful as possible with the rear brake. Any front end slide will probably receive instant involuntary response. It is unlikely that both wheels will find the lock up point at the same instant. If they do, luck is about all that will help. With quick enough reactions such a situation may just escape turning into an accident. Not something you can rely on, however, so once again the rule is not to let it happen in the first place by being more aware and better practised.

In addition to the rubbery feeling described above, some tyres begin to squeal just before lock up. With signs as powerful as these, hard braking moves out of the unknown and becomes a useful, essential ally.

Once you have gained some of the skills necessary for hard braking find a nice, tight corner and practise leaving your braking as late as possible. This is where the real fun starts. Ideally, braking should be over and done with at around the point where you begin to peel into the corner. If this ideal situation is missed it will be necessary to continue braking into and around the corner. Not to be recommended, we will be examining this situation in chapter seven. At the moment, keep practising late, late braking.

Motorcycles are at their least manoeuverable under heavy braking. Which is fine if it is into a safe, predictable corner, less so in an

On some bikes the engine braking takes a little getting used to

emergency. Steering becomes very heavy with all the weight forcing forward and changes of direction are difficult. Again, chapter seven will give pointers on how to steer better under braking. For the moment, remember to make allowances.

One of the inherent weaknesses of current motorcycle design is the lack of suspension under braking. Compressing the forks stiffens the suspension and reduces the forks' capacity to cope with bumps. Modern anti-dive systems are finding their way onto some road machines but do not really do what their names implies. Their real strength is to help the machine cope with bumps in the early stages of hard braking, or throughout the whole process of normal braking.

The greatest danger related to the difficulties of the front suspension is that with a fully compressed suspension, a bump can take sufficient weight off the front end to begin a slide. Usually, such bumps provoke a small squeal from the tyre and braking continues. Beware of more disastrous happenings however.

If your machine's forks are not properly damped a bump or pothole may prompt front wheel patter. In extreme circumstances, simply braking hard can start this off, in which case a thorough overhaul of the front suspension is in order.

Cope with wheel patter, as usual, by releasing all the front brake and then re-applying. Its onset is signalled by a severe vibration from the front of the bike. In fact, as the forks have compressed their springs, inadequate damping has allowed them to rebound slightly. The increasing weight of braking pushes the forks down again, they bounce, and so on. Unless caught early on wheel patter will inevitably lead to a sliding front wheel. If wheel patter does occur with a modern machine it will undoubtedly signal that there is a severe deficiency in the machine, such as insufficient or incorrect fork oil.

Another regular failing on modern machines is the drive chain. Without frequent and regular attention and lubrication, chains can play a part in reducing braking efficiency.

Braking hard suddenly takes all the drive out of the chain. If it is too slack the chain will begin to slop up and down, jerking at the rear sprocket. This jerking will add to the braking effect of the rear wheel in a totally unpredictable manner, possibly provoking a slide.

However competent you become at braking it is worthless if you are not ready to use it. Make sure you are and stay alive.

6 Winding it out

Nothing sums up the excitement of motor-cycling more than acceleration. Stretching the throttle wires and pointing the front wheel skywards is one sure way of getting the adrenalin pumping.

You could be forgiven for thinking nothing could be easier than screwing open the twist-grip and generally getting crazy. Largely, you would be right but like everything else about two wheeled excitement practice improves the process. Which in this case means you go faster and increase the thrills. Which can't be bad.

Just like anything that generates kicks, danger lurks everywhere. Acceleration puts stresses through the frame and suspension, changing subtly the expected performance and predictability of the machine. Largely, however, acceleration is less risk prone than other motorcycling extremes.

To cap all this, extremes of acceleration lead to wheelies as the back wheel rushes to overtake the front one. With modern developments in motorcycle design, not just in engine performance but in frame geometry and tyre technology as well, the wheelie has quickly entered every hard riding motorcyclist's vocabulary. Just as it has entered day to day language, so must the wheelie enter the armoury of skills a good rider must command. Once there, it needs to be developed in preparation for the day when, unexpectedly, the front wheel hops off the ground. The practised rider will think little of the situation. Unsure and unready, an inexperienced rider could easily

be surprised and turn a potentially safe situation into a lethal disaster.

As most will already know, just about every motorcycle will accelerate, initially at least, quicker than any other vehicle on the road. Particularly with larger machines, such blistering acceleration is at once a thrill and a danger. With practice and good sense the danger will recede.

In most public road situations, particularly in traffic, it is foolish to suggest that unrestrained acceleration is appropriate. What is necessary is a knowledge of your machine's performance and the ability constantly and accurately to predict the reaction of the machine to the road in front. Under acceleration the bike changes geometry and reacts differently. We must integrate the machine behavioural changes in our riding technique and anticipation.

Already, following the back to basics examination of throttle and clutch in chapter three, you should be moving towards extracting every last drop of performance from your motorcycle. In that chapter, we considered this action from the point of view of machine controls and rider sensitivity. Now we must consider relating those lessons to the road.

Hard acceleration seems to have only been associated with pulling away from rest. A combination of drag racing and a concentration on quarter mile times by the motorcycle press and manufacturers are probably to blame but in road going reality giving it stick from stationary happens rarely compared to

Winding it on through a corner

the number of miles travelled. In many more instances acceleration will be from one speed to another but, first things first, let's examine pulling away.

Most machines will manage the wrench from rest to sixty miles an hour in under five seconds. Some bikes will considerably reduce even this short time, particularly superbikes. For all the superiority of such times compared to the motorcar—a result of the favourable power to weight ratio of the motorcycle—only two wheels and a high centre of gravity are responsible for the likely instabilities of an accelerating motorcycle.

Wheelspin will probably be familiar to anyone who has pulled away on a slippy surface, particularly in wet weather. Correction will have been a reflex reaction, probably before you were even aware of what was happening. In wet weather wheelspin will happen at low speeds and relatively gentle rates of acceleration. Catching the rear wheel is achieved by shutting off the throttle and re-establishing direct tyre contact with the road surface. Don't shut off quickly enough could find you in another kind of direct contact with the road surface!

In the dry, however, wheelspin is caused by another of the motorcycle's design compromises. For maximum grip the rider wants as

Open it up . . .

. . . and a little bit more

much weight as possible on the rear wheel. So the rider sits as directly over the rear wheel as he can. Except that now, the front end is so light that wheelies occur too easily. Fun though they are, wheelies do not help rapid progress. In typical road conditions, keeping the front end down will be more important than putting weight over the rear wheel. Although some machine weight is thrown backwards when accelerating, just as weight comes forward under braking, a combination of factors make this a less effective grip seeking phenomenon.

Leaning forward to counteract a lifting front end, you must expect the onset of wheelspin. Get used to the bike and try to predict just when wheelspin is about to occur. At this point you will be getting maximum traction and the most drive.

Even on loose or slippy surfaces wheelspin is unlikely to present any great dangers. Most bikes will stay quite naturally in line, perhaps guided with a little input. A wheelspinning machine will try and 'fishtail' sideways but this is easily countered by the rider keeping the handlebars held straight and persuading the machine in the right direction by use of bodyweight. For such dramatic behaviour there can be no hard and fast rules and anyway on normal road bikes such activity is only likely to last briefly. In the wet, searching for any sort of absolute limit is foolish. A wet road surface has no predictability—don't trust it. Powering through wheelspin in such conditions can only mean trouble.

Once things are moving at a respectable pace wheelspin can be forgotten. Except in the most extreme circumstances it will never occur other than during the muscular wrench from rest.

Shut off to return to earth

If good traction is found from the back wheel then a hard charge off the line may provoke the motorcycle's last statement of defiance—the wheelie. Some machines combine weight distribution, frame geometry and power characteristics to lift the front wheel at the least invitation. Others refuse to shake off weight from the front and go aviating. Those of the bikes that pop up easily need only a vigorously open throttle for life to become interesting. Most machines only wheelie with a certain amount of encouragement. Some motorcycles, of course, are so heavy and cumbersome as to be downright impossible to pull up.

The more right thinking among us would say it's difficult to see the need for such excitable behaviour but motorcycles are there to be enjoyed and mastered, so why ignore wheelies? They are not necessarily dangerous, however the bike is in such a potentially unstable condition with only one wheel on the ground that good sense should tell you when it is safe to have a go.

The one thing that keeps most of us from taking the chance—popping the clutch and, as a result, the front wheel—is fear. A legitimate one, too, of damaging probably your only form of personal transport. For there can often be nothing so expensive as a wonky wheelie in terms of machine as well as personal damage. If you seriously aim to be one of the daredevil few who monowheel confidently for yards at a time, be prepared for hours of practice; lots of bruises; the risk of more serious personal damage and quite a bit of money in machine repairs. The best possible way to practise is on an old, light bike well away from the public highway in a trail park or a friendly farmer's field. Make sure you are well protected with boots, gloves and tough clothes because a tumbling motorcycle has a lot of sharp edges.

It is difficult to provide simple guidelines on how to achieve perfect wheelies. Everyone seems to use different techniques but there are some rules which begin to emerge.

Primarily, keep looking where you are going. This may sound a little odd but most trainee monowheelers quickly find a considerable fascination in the front wheel. However, the wheel cannot be lifted by staring at it. So look ahead and leave your sense of feel to balance things for you.

Next thing to realise is that on one wheel not only do you need to keep an eye on front to rear balance but that side to side balance becomes far more difficult. As the front wheel rises so does the centre of gravity of the machine. Imagine trying to balance your bike sitting on a seat three feet higher than normal and you will realise how much concentration is necessary to keep a monowheeling machine upright.

If you are still keen after all those warnings, read on. Ultimately, the aim will be to balance the machine on the rear wheel for as long as you like. Begin by gradually pulling up the front wheel higher and higher for brief periods. To start with, stand on the footpegs to improve balance. As you improve you can then begin to sit down. To pull up the front wheel ride with the engine turning on the lower edge of the power band in first or second gear. Briefly roll off the throttle, moving weight forward at the same time then open it up quickly. As you do so and the bike begins to accelerate quickly move your body weight backwards, gently pulling the handlebars up as you go. Synchronise the springing upwards of the front forks, acceleration and redistribution of weight properly and the front wheel will aviate quite easily.

Use of throttle plays its part in cornering

In the end it's all good fun, in the right place

Wheelies are best sustained by pulling the wheel up when the bike is on the move, rather than trying to pop straight up from rest. Slipping the clutch is difficult in the beginning with so much to think about so it is better to rely on engine torque to lift the bike. As you become more accustomed to motorcycles up on one wheel concentrate on the search for balance. Once you begin to get a little confidence readjust your technique to use less weight transfer, concentrating more on the natural acceleration of the machine. This change of emphasis will eventually allow you to remain on the seat.

Always cover the rear brake once you have begun to settle down since this is the only way to bring down the front wheel if things begin to get wayward. Those are the basics. Be prepared for lots of practice before you begin to approach the standard set by some of the specialists. Above all, keep practising only in a safe environment well away from traffic.

Most riders will make do with the odd short, powered wheelie rather than the unending practice and risk in anything more ambitious.

Once moving along at a reasonable pace acceleration becomes the preserve of the motorcycle's power rather than the efforts of the rider. As we have said smoothness and sympathy for the bike will help acceleration. In particular, being in the right gear is essential. Riders used to small machines who find themselves in charge of a larger machine will often feel uneasy about changing down at high speed. Most superbikes are capable of clearing 100 mph not just in top gear but often in lower gears as well. Changing down at 110 to accelerate may seem dramatic but if full performance is wanted that is the only way to get it.

Acceleration is easy to enjoy. It has become the yardstick by which we judge our machines. However much acceleration we have, riders will become used to it and ready for more. Already bikes are providing stunning acceleration. Perhaps it is time to find enjoyment from other aspects of motorcyling.

7 So this is what it is all about

Throwing down the gauntlet in chapter one this book has taken you through balance, braking and acceleration. Finally, we are ready to talk about cornering, something every rider can appreciate.

Although this aspect of motorcyling can be enjoyed by anyone it is the single least understood element in the riding process. Too often, through a lack of appreciation, hauling a motorcycle around corners is one which receives little regard. Motorcycles do not steer straightforwardly like cars. Rather, there is a combination of factors which contribute to the steering process. Only by separating out each of these factors, examining them closely individually and then building a coherent, flowing style will a rider be able to prove his abilities. For most people improvement will not be a matter of small degree. Far too many will be able to make vast improvement by following a few simple rules.

Needless to say, cornering introduces all manner of dangers. However good you become tanking around corners at a rapid rate never ride beyond visible limits. The risks are too great to charge into a blind bend at 60 mph, knowing that you would be unable to stop if something suddenly blocked your way. Never become fully committed to a corner without being secure in the knowledge that the way ahead is clear.

Cornering places sideways thrusts on a motorcycle's tyres with which the rider needs to familiarise himself gradually. Different tyres naturally enough exhibit changing character-istics. Some have excellent grip but slide very suddenly while others begin to slide predictably but too early. You may be lucky and have tyres with both the desirable features of high grip and predictability or be lumbered with hopeless treads in all conditions. Unfortunately, not many of us are in a position to pick and choose which tyres are best by trial and error. Once we have a set of tyres they stay on the bike until they are worn out and they can be changed. So whatever tyres are on your machine you will probably have to learn to live with them.

Nothing is more unpredictable than an under-inflated tyre so keep pressures well checked according to the maker's specification. Recognise that the performance of a tyre will change as it wears. For sports riding, round section tyres are the ideal, keeping an equal amount of grip on the road at any angle of lean. Unfortunately tyres wear out predominantly down the middle, flattening the profile of the tyre. This is fine when you are rolling along in a straight line but as you begin to turn you may find the bike turning on the ridge created where the flattened centre strip meets the less worn sides of the tyres. Up on this ridge there is far less tread on the road than there was when the tyre was new, so take care. Some rear tyres are actually made square in section and tipping these up on their corners is not recommended. But you could probably get away with it—just proceed with caution.

Motorcycles become easily manoeuverable

Shifting bodyweight helps cornering

as soon as steering principles are learned and applied with skill. Contrary to popular belief motorcycles are steered—not simply thought around corners. Most people, questioned closely on how they actually get around corners, reply with a weak 'lean it over'. For a good rider all changes of direction will consciously begin with the handlebars, complemented by other actions.

Above all, those riders unfamiliar with the basic steering principle of a motorcycle will be disconcerted to learn that for all but the slowest speeds, turning a motorcycle to the right actually involves turning the handlebars to the left.

Before concentrating too hard on that particular revelation let's examine slow speed turning. As you plough your way through traffic, steering a motorcycle is effected by similar principles to those which apply to a car. As you turn the handlebars to the right,

It doesn't show, but steering right tilts you over to the left

too quickly, with you uncertain each time whether safety would be achieved around the bend or disaster would strike before you made it. Gradually you became more confident as your subconscious came into play, registering each body movement and the resulting machine reaction. As experience built up, barriers were pushed back until today, when you ride in complete confidence but unsure and unaware of any absolute limits.

Those first few uncertain corners took place before your subconscious and developing experience found the transition point between steering right to go right and the unexpected steering left to go right as speed increased. Without conscious practice and development your riding technique is probably still locked into this sort of remembered reaction experience.

Once riders reach their early twenties insurance companies recognise them as an infinitely safer risk and premiums come tumbling down. The onset of age combines experience with an unwillingness to experiment which leads to a safe riding formula at a reasonable but unexceptional standard. Which seems a shame because the true satisfaction of motorcycling must be complete mastery of the complex process of cornering.

By consciously examining the cornering learning process new riders could be taught a few guidelines on how to steer, helping them avoid some of those wilderness years of experiment. Helping them, perhaps, to avoid those painful bumps and scrapes which at the moment are considered to be part of growing up—but too often stop them from growing up at all.

Older, more experienced riders should begin to experiment again, this time within properly defined limits and discover the real thrills of riding in complete control. There are many other areas involved in safe motorcycling

say, the changed attitude of the front tyre's contact patch creates a different friction area which takes the front end around to the right. This will subconsciously be combined with a small lean to the right. Sure enough, the bike goes around the corner. However, at some indefinable moment just a few mph faster such action becomes inadequate.

Think back to the days when you first began riding. Sitting on your first real motorcycle, no doubt slightly awed by its size, it seemed a pretty wayward beast. The cornering ability of the first bike seemed fairly limited and more often than not corners loomed up

On slower turns the front wheel will turn inwards

necessary. Braking begins although not a great deal is required since the corner is a quick one. While braking you pop the bike down into the right gear. At the peel off point on the left of the available roadway you apply firm pressure to pull the bars to the left. This effectively throws the weight of the bike over to the right. Once tracking correctly around the required radius the bars are left to find their own position, running with the corner. As the exit arrives it's time to straighten up again and the bike is stood up quickly by tugging the bars to the right. Full power can now be squirted on as you hurry towards the next corner.

If you have never been aware of this process before, introduce yourself to it gently. After even a little practice you will be amazed at the added control this gives and how much further ahead it allows you to think. Begin playing with this technique without changing any other riding habits. After all, new techniques demand experiment to introduce them and every experiment involves a degree of risk. On the other hand, without experiment nothing improves.

Once reverse steering becomes a conscious and integral part of your riding it is time to consider and improve the other factors which influence motorcycle steering.

If you have survived so far without being aware of reverse steering then you will almost certainly have been using shifts of body weight to corner your motorcycle. Although unsatisfactory on its own, when used in conjunction with good steering body weight transfer gives useful assistance and aids control. Basically as the handlebar input knocks the bike off balance the rider aids this imbalance by shifting his own weight in the

which we will examine later but greater directional control must be central to improved safety.

'Leaning it over' is no answer to the problems outlined above—that is what happens, not how. Mention has been made of the opposite steering principle so take a closer look at how motorcycle tracks around a corner.

Imagine a long straight running into a fast 90 degree right hander with a similar straight at the exit. Visibility is good, the surface dry and problem free. There is no other traffic. You are riding a powerful machine and are no doubt planning to take the corner at good speed in reasonable style and with a minimum of risk.

As the bend approaches some braking is

Slower turns don't need such dramatic shifts of bodyweight

. . . pull bars hard to the right, throwing the bike over to the left . . .

. . . to exit with the power on

direction of the turn. We are really venturing into the realms of personal preference when discussing this weight transfer and you must give consideration to developing a personal style which answers all the necessary requirements rather than trying to emulate your favourite superstar.

There are several ways to move body weight on a motorcycle. The first of these is to leave legs and feet stationary and to lean the torso only. No doubt you will have seen pictures of people who ride like this and thought they looked rather odd. To achieve maximum leverage with this limited movement usually makes the rider sit as upright as possible which looks awkward compared

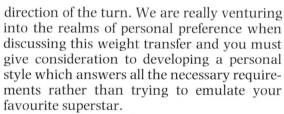

The traffic island sequence . . . lean to the right, then . . .

to the more normal hunching forward into the wind style. On its own this is not a particularly effective way of steering the bike but together with precise, handlebar initiated steering can give an increased feeling of security.

Pushing down hard on the relevant footpeg can also have some effect on steering but in most circumstances will be pretty ineffectual and redundant. This technique does lead to that most familiar of weight shifting styles, hanging out of the saddle.

Up to now we have not considered moving in the saddle at all but it will become an increasingly important facet of riding. Once you have moved out of the centrally seated position the motorcycle will permanently be trying to corner. Only through handlebar input is it prevented from doing so until the appropriate moment.

It usually takes a long time to get used to the hang off style and some riders will never find it satisfactory. Give it a good try and don't be put off too quickly and you may suddenly find it all comes right and your riding has improved considerably.

Hanging off involves standing on the pegs and shifting across the saddle in the direction of the bend. Some riders adopt the position

Stability through sensitivity

Make adjustments to the cornering line through the handlebars

before the corner, others actually use this movement to aid leaning the bike at the instant when reverse steering is begun. This last action is probably the 'purest' since hanging off before the corner will demand some correction through the handlebars until the peel off point is reached. The decision as to which particular method suits you best must remain a personal one.

69

Once hanging off, the familiar knee sticking out stance will be found to be the most natural, to force as much weight as far out as possible. Sticking your knee out should never be seen as anything other than a by-product of shifting weight out of the saddle.

Opinion is divided on the benefits of hanging off a motorcycle. Some of the all-time heroes of racing remain firmly in the seat apparently unmoving from the start of a race to the finish. Others scramble from side to side with equally effective results. There is a claim that hanging off reduces the necessary amount of lean for a given radius. This is to some extent true but not for the expected reasons. It must be recognised that in cornering the rider must seek the least angle of lean to be most effective. Less capable riders often find themselves leaning over further but going no faster as a result of poor coordination of steering input and weight transfer. Hanging off makes it easier to find the optimum lean angle, making the rider feel he is cornering better. Such improvements only come with lots of practice and some riders will never be happy hanging off a cornering machine. Also, if things get a little out of hand with a slide the inexperienced rider will find it difficult to correct such problems from an extreme position on one side of the motorcycle.

Hanging off the bike will no doubt continue to provoke discussion and advocates of the technique for road use are equally likely to be accused of posing. It really is a case of taking the old saying 'If it feels right, do it' and practising accordingly.

Once the motorcycle is cornering it is often necessary to make slight corrections to miss unforeseen potholes or allow for a tightening bend. Almost without exception this is best achieved by input from the handlebars rather than trying to readjust rider bodyweight. Balancing the bike while hanging from it seems to aid this correction procedure with the rider more relaxed.

Equally, hanging off seems to help the rider cope with the hops and wobbles of the machine, feeling he can allow such activity to go on below and beside him without it ever becoming a threat to his safety. It gives an improved sense of balance. For the rider who cannot get to grips with the hanging off technique a similar result can be achieved by sticking both knees out. Most of these ploys are psychological tricks to make the rider feel more in control. There's nothing wrong with that as long as it does not make things any more dangerous.

Having gone through steering technique you should now be in a position to get great fun from a good, tight S-bend. At the point of crossover such bends demand a hefty wrench on the bars in the opposite direction to the forthcoming corner to throw the machine up over the vertical and down on the other side for the next bend. This up and over sequence appears to have the effect of lightening the bike and rider thus 'throwing' both up in the air slightly. The only warning for this is the corresponding lack of grip which can be expected. If possible try to make any such manoeuvre follow two distinct phases—up to the vertical and then down for the next bend. This gives the suspension and hence tyre grip the chance to catch up. Exiting from an island involves this sort of action, usually right where the inward camber of the roundabout meets the opposite slope of the exit road. This introduces a ridge in the road surface at the point where the bike is already lightened with the effect of risking even greater grip problems for the tyres. So watch out next time you go scratching round your favourite roundabout and dive for the exit in the grand manner.

Approach tyre limits gradually

On tight turns, the front wheel will run with the bend

Braking around corners is often held to be the most heinous crime of all and will unavoidably end in complete disaster. While it may not be the safest thing in the world it can be done and should never be dismissed as impossible. You never know when it might be the only way out.

Braking into a corner can continue for some time since the extra weight thrown forward with the machine upright will remain pressed downward, improving front tyre grip well into the bend. The risk is that lessened rear grip will allow the back wheel to slide away.

Moving to change gear while cornering

Once the machine is cornering normally without brakes then any kind of panic stopping is impossible without prior straightening up. A gentle slowing can be achieved although this is only likely to be necessary in emergencies or as a result of an error of judgement. When cornering, weight is thrown down onto the tyres. This changes the principle of using brakes and the aim must be to use equal amounts of braking front and rear though never using enough to provoke a slide. In a panic stop, straighten the bike up quickly with reverse steering before applying any

brakes and then hope you have enough tarmac on which to stop.

In particular, treat the front brake with caution. Although instantaneous front wheel slides can be tolerated in a straight line, round corners you would be really lucky to get away with it. The same applies to the rear brake—over-harsh use will certainly have unpleasant results.

Acceleration plays a fundamental part in effective cornering. The very process of cornering has the effect of scrubbing off power so, in theory, if you entered a bend at a given speed and maintained constant throttle throughout, on exit you would be travelling slower. That effect and the fact that it's good fun powering out of bends as fast as possible demand good throttle use when cornering.

Usually, the acceleration process will begin about a quarter of the way around the bend immediately after the braking is finished. Gently at first allowing the suspension to find a reasonable equilibrium after braking, acceleration will build up until full power will be used on the exit. The risks of too much power are obvious—the rear end steps out. If you are inexperienced at leaning over, and lack of opportunity puts many people in this category, rear end slides are sometimes difficult to recognise until it's too late. Strange though this may sound, when leaned over at particularly radical angles the detection of a rear wheel slide becomes quite difficult and will only become easier with experience. If you are determined to come out of corners faster than anyone else get used to the technique of applying power at extreme angles gently.

Acceleration introduces favourable tensions into the machine apparently aiding its stability when cornering. In addition to this

Look as far ahead as you can

Keep in tight on the exit

some riders further improve stability by trailing the rear brake as they power through corners. This may sound contradictory, accelerating with the brake on, but it's not as daft as it sounds. A very lightly applied rear brake can go some way toward keeping the rear tyre in firmer contact with the road. If you reach such a point where this technique becomes necessary you are probably going too fast for the public road anyway and it is time you found a racetrack.

In chapter five we found that a slack drive chain can lock the rear wheel when braking. This situation can be disastrous if you are a late braker and it occurs when the bike is well cranked over. If you do find chain snatch occuring, and again this is only likely to happen at a racetrack, the answer is to keep the chain in positive tension by maintaining a little throttle and not shutting off entirely when entering a bend. Remember that too much throttle will seriously affect the brakes.

It should not really need to be said that any kind of controlled slide has absolutely no place on the public road. Surfaces are nowhere near predictable enough; road bike tyre technology is in no way adequate and the need for quick reactions is considerably increased. Don't do it.

On some long, sweeping bends it often becomes necessary to change up a gear. This

Check the best line is clear before becoming fully committed

need not cause great alarm but it does demand special care. Even the best gear changes will involve power being cut off momentarily. The combination of power pulling the bike upright and rider persuading it to stay leaning into the corner is thrown into confusion. The bike will want to lie down into the corner and will only be snatched away from toppling over completely as power is reapplied. This fluctuation can be, depending on the motorcycle, sufficient to tie the suspension into knots and set off almost terminal wobbles and shakes. Be aware that this could well be the case and counteract the expected reaction. Just before the gearchange, roll the throttle slightly and run the bike at constant power. This will take some of the pretensioning out of the suspension. At the point of changing gear adopt a neutral steering position and reduce if possible any off-set weight by pushing down on the outer foot-peg. This can be a little tricky if the outside peg also carries the gearchange.

The minor uneasiness often caused by changing gear while cornering is hardly ever terminal but since it can provoke some unsettling wobbles it is worth taking steps to minimise the effects. Some machines are more prone to confusion from such action than others so above all don't worry about something which may not even exist.

Cornering, as we said at the beginning,

holds the substance of the enjoyment of motorcycling. Wheelies, stoppies and wheel-spin all contribute an exciting veneer but the real satisfaction lies in the concentration required for successful, rapid bend swinging. Unfortunately a mythology has built up which drives some of the inexperienced to try too hard while others cover up and say they know what happens without ever really understanding. Both riders lose out. The former because he is taking risks so great they should never be considered and the latter because he is held back by false fears.

Learning and improving technique can only occur when you are sufficiently self critical to assess your own riding ability truthfully. No-one else can do it for you.

Once you really understand cornering, corners beginning to blend together and footpegs brushing the blacktop with increasing regularity, take your enthusiasm to the racetrack to develop advanced technique. There is a limit within most people's reach as to just how quickly you can go on public roads before being at continuously excessive risk. Learn to find this point, then don't go beyond it.

8 Putting it together

Just how good a rider you really are will depend on how well you blend the contents of the previous chapters into your riding style. As will already be clear, to develop a good style will demand a considerable amount of self criticism. Even if you are not prepared to admit to it in public, privately bottle up the ego before letting yourself loose with horsepower.

Building the right approach will take time. Pushing back your own performance limits in areas we have talked through must be done gently, a little at a time. Above all, good riding demands the right mental approach—constant concentration and awareness. A competent rider fully in control of his motorcycle with this concentrated thinking to help him will travel quicker and infinitely more safely than the street racer whose sole objective is to impress. That's not to say don't go scratching. Just think about it when you do.

As you become more thoughtful about your riding you will become more aware of areas of technique which feel awkward. They do not feel right and intrude on an otherwise smooth performance. It may be that changing down gears while braking or the whole operation of the right hand feels difficult. Keep trying with such difficulties and with concentration you will be surprised at how quickly previously messy actions become more efficient and blend in with the rest of your riding style.

On public roads hazards lie around every corner and behind every tree. Other vehicles simply make things worse. When something does get in the way and threatens your safety no amount of incredible technique will save you unless reaction times are up to the job. Through constant concentration and anticipation you can reduce this mental delay to a minimum. More importantly, by proper concentration you are more likely to take the correct action rather than be panicked into making matters worse.

In general riding the importance of reaction times is reduced by anticipation taking over. Braking points, for instance, can be planned in advance and action taken at the appropriate moment. However, every action of the rider conscious or otherwise is subject to a reaction time. By employing good concentration you can be sure of reducing this delay to a minimum. Once the required blend of concentration and awareness is discovered a kind of uneasiness settles over riders when they are pushing their luck. In short, they have discovered how to relate their reaction time and likely stopping distance to the visible road ahead.

Experienced riders may sometimes complain of having a bad day when nothing seems to go right. This is often more than bad luck. Tiredness, colds or mild flu can slow reaction times considerably. With slowed reactions the public highway can suddenly become a very dangerous place, particularly for a rider used to travelling quite quickly trying to maintain his usual pace.

A slow reaction time will obviously extend stopping distances or delay taking action. What is not so apparent is that the quality of

Develop a smooth style

the decision over what to do will also be affected by a sluggish brain. In addition the ability to steer or brake will not be as sharp as it might be.

Intensely cold weather will also provoke a slowing effect on reaction times. Never allow yourself to get too cold during the winter. If it means stopping to start the circulation going again do so. Never continue to ride if you have started to shiver as once this point has been reached an accident could be over before you have reacted.

A good long day's riding is the love of many motorcyclists. Sustaining the necessary concentration can become a problem on such journeys as tiredness creeps in at the end of the day. A tired motorcyclist is one with slow reactions and one that finds it difficult to stay alert. After, say, a day at a race meeting with a long journey home think about these effects and allow for them.

On long trips it's worth keeping an eye on the speedometer. The human failure to perceive speed after a period of riding is well known but difficult to overcome. After sustained motorway cruising, 30 mph seems like walking pace. This can, unless you are careful, lead to errors of judgement at corners or junctions. This false perception of speed also has the effect of gradually increasing the average speed of a rider over a long day. Coupled with the usual anxiety to get home, this can lead to faster and faster speeds just as reaction times and ability are at their lowest ebb—not a particularly healthy combination.

While considering reaction times it is worth mentioning that other road users suffer from exactly the same problems as does the motorcyclist. In fact, the motorcyclist is so constantly aware of the dangers around him that his reactions are usually better than those of fellow road users.

Don't rely on others to make decisions for you. Always allow plenty of room for error.

Riding properly demands that wherever possible the rider is following the correct cornering line. On the racetrack the racing line is plain to see as the rider uses every inch of available space to straighten out corners. To a lesser extent, this technique can improve road riding skills as well. Naturally, to shift around bends at a good rate demands that some bend straightening is useful but there are other advantages.

Consider the racing motorcyclist approaching a right hander. He moves his machine well to the left of the available track and runs deep into the corner before peeling off rapidly to the right. At about the mid point of the corner the motorcycle will run close to the right hand kerb before swinging out wide to the left on exit.

Notice that the racer will run deep into the corner before starting to turn. Most people would find such action difficult at first, requiring a conscious resistance of the temptation to wander over to the right of the track too early. By leaning into a corner earlier than absolutely necessary, the machine will be leaning longer than it has to and thus unable to accelerate or brake to the maximum. Likewise on exit most riders would find themselves wandering out of the corner somewhere around the middle of the track.

Most public roads carry traffic in two directions, however, so unless the road is visibly clear for a long way ahead only one half can be used. Public roads are usually further complicated by having potholes and drain covers at their sides; raised white lines apparently designed to have the maximum upsetting effect on motorcycles; and peculiar cambers which usually contrive to increase the effec-

Safely enjoying the freedom of the road

Cornering brings out motorcycling's attractions

Riding quickly, relaxed and alert

tive angle of lean of a motorcycle, reducing the expected grip.

Using all the available road gives obvious assistance to those who wish to corner as fast as is reasonable. In addition there are other, more useful benefits for the road rider. By keeping well to the appropriate side on approaching a bend and running deep into it before peeling off, the road rider is afforded the best possible view around the forthcoming bend before he is completely committed to it. Hazards, moving or stationary, will be visible far earlier than if the rider was positioned further out in the road before the corner. In the event of a vehicle travelling in the opposite direction losing control, that vehicle will run wide on the exit assuming it managed to get that far in the first place. The well-positioned rider will be in the safest place, farthest away from the erratic vehicle.

One further word about driving deep into the corner before peeling off. Allowing yourself to drift out towards the apex of the bend too early will involve riding closer to the traffic coming the other way for a longer period.

Keeping a racing line minimises the risk from other traffic, provides a better view of the road ahead and allows the corner to be taken quicker. All in all, that seems to make it a useful technique.

Throughout a riding career, most motorcyclists will be lucky enough to ride several machines of widely varying capacity and capability. During the first ride on any strange machine there will be a brief period during which the controls and feel of the machine will be alien. Brakes may seem grabby or inadequate; the clutch stiffer than normal; or the throttle may feel strange. Every rider, however experienced, will need a period of familiarisation before being able to trust the machine and approach anything like its performance limits. It is foolish to treat this period with contempt and rush straight to the redline in every gear, howling the front tyre to every stop. Some machines demand a different approach, they need to be synchronised with a particular style. Even if you are lucky enough to survive a hell-for-leather approach to unfamiliar machinery you will miss whatever innate character that particular machine possesses. Take time to introduce yourself to new machinery.

Inevitably, most riders will one day find themselves riding more powerful machinery to that which they have previously been accustomed. This will be part of the natural progression from the small machine on which most initial learning was done to the kind of machine to which any sporting rider gravitates. Bigger in size and definitely more powerful, such motorcycles cannot be approached without being prepared to start learning different techniques. Broadly the heavier a bike the more consciously it needs to be steered.

Some may make the graduation to larger machines in small steps, others will make a straight jump from small machine to superbike. Obviously the latter will feel the difference far more than the former. A large increase in performance takes some time to get

On the road, companions together

used to. Acceleration will never seem to end even from motorway plus speeds. Acclimatization to this new, enormous surge will be quick enough. What will be more difficult to get used to will be where all this acceleration and power can get you—higher speeds.

Opportunities to extend powerful machines to their upper performance limits are fairly infrequent and for someone unfamiliar with high speed can seem fairly hair raising. Like most things, speeds which initially seemed unbelievable and on the verge of uncontrollability soon lose their fears. The eyes have simply become acclimatised to the extra speed.

Previous page **Absorbed by the road ahead**

Don't ignore safety, but do enjoy yourself

Although you may become confident at very high speed, remember that others may not be able to cope with you, approaching from behind at twice their speed. Oncoming drivers will be unfamiliar with such speed and may make misjudgements as to your arrival rate. Whatever the injustice, to travel fast and safely the rider must always expect the worst and think as far ahead as possible. At a combined approach speed of 140 mph a driver's hesitation or a moment's bad judgement 300 yards up the road can spell disaster for an approaching motorcyclist. Never become blasé about speed.

Although speed may become a familiar commodity for the owner of any superbike, it must be accepted that everyone has an absolute speed limit, beyond which human reactions and judgement are simply not quick enough to provide adequate warning and avoidance tactics at hazards. However important it may be to ride fast, it is worth remembering that fact.

It must be apparent by now that there are two occasions when the notion of riding fast has to be locked away firmly and good sense takes over—at night and in the wet. A third could be when there are policemen about, but we won't go into that!

In the wet, with perfect vision usually impossible through a wet visor or goggles and completely unpredictable road surfaces liberally coated with diesel and other spewed-out lubricants, the limitations of two wheeled travel become apparent. At quite low speeds slides will occur so even the most insensitive clod will soon recognise the danger of exceeding a reasonable pace.

On a dry night, the dangers can be less apparent but the simple fact is that accident rates rise steeply after dark. Fatigue sets in far

Comfortably cruising

quicker after dark, travelling as the rider is in lower night time temperatures and straining his eyes to pick up as much detail as possible. Reaction times are consequently liable to drop with all the effects mentioned earlier. It's worth making a mental note of where the light switch is on a strange machine. On some bikes without day-lights permanently running it is quite easy to find total darkness when all you were looking for was high beam. Great fun at 70 mph.

Although the headlights of advancing vehicles warn of potential hazards, don't forget that not all hazards have headlights. Pedestrians, animals—often paralysed by approaching headlights—and potholes in the road are familiar problems so ride within the capability of your own headlights. Oncoming headlights, even on dip beam, can blind you particularly if your visor is getting a bit old. Keep the visor in good condition and never look directly at advancing headlights but do use the advantage they give of lighting up more road than your own lights.

Pulling all the loose ends of techniques and a realistic approach will be a satisfying process. Develop a good, flowing style under safe conditions and then extend it to encompass advanced techniques. Constantly check for lapses in your standard and always try to learn more from experience and playing around. Ride within your own personal limits and those of surrounding motorists. Mental, physical and mechanical preparation will pay dividends in increased peace of mind, safety and enjoyment.

Do not dismiss official safety advice as officious, governmental and legalistic propaganda designed to curtail the freedom of the individual. Most of it is good advice and the rest tells you what is legal and what isn't. Always remember that when you are riding outside the rules whatever happens must be your own fault. The main aim of riding a motorcycle is for enjoyment and excitement. Make sure you attain and continue to attain both.

9 Passengers, passengers

Most motorcycles are designed and built with performance in mind. Performance motorcycles are not seen as anything more than a solo machine so it is hardly surprising that pillion passenger accommodation seems to be tagged on as an afterthought. With only a grudging regard for the expected suspension and geometry changes a passenger imposes, designers leave it to the rider and his long-suffering passenger to manage as best they can.

On a vehicle so relatively light as a motorcycle, adding the weight of a passenger will obviously change the whole balance and approach of the motorcycle. It is the rider's responsibility to take the right action to make sure that things stay safe—any passenger muffled up inside a helmet sitting behind the rider places their safety entirely in his hands.

Adding a passenger on the back of a motorcycle has one very obvious effect—the rear suspension is compressed. As this happens the front wheel will, to some extent, be lightened relative to the rear. Already, viewed from this superficial angle all that has previously been said about the balance of a motorcycle and how that affects braking has been upset. No longer can you rely on the front brake to generate 80 per cent of the stopping power or the front tyre to provide the same amount of grip. On top of all this, the load on the back is probably nervous and wobbling, seemingly with its own definite ideas on where the motorcycle should be directed.

First of all, the passenger needs a thorough briefing on how to ride the perfect pillion.

Assuming your passenger is a novice, they will probably be nervous. After all, they may be putting their life in your hands. If you are not sure whether or not your passenger has ridden before, ask them. Even if they already have some passenger experience it's worth running through good procedure and letting them know a little about your likely riding technique. Best advice at this point is to tell your passenger to try to be an inanimate bundle of luggage, firmly strapped on the back seat. Don't tell them they look like this, they might get upset.

Spend time explaining that once on the move, your novice passenger should sit still without making any sudden movements.

Above all, explain that when a corner arrives you will be leaning the bike over. The passenger should just relax and keep his body in a straight line with the machine. Nothing is worse than riding into the first corner with a frightened passenger, only to find they insist on sitting upright, struggling to keep the motorcycle in the same attitude. Usually you can allow your passenger to move their head around without worrying you too much so they can at least admire the view when their nerves will allow.

Suggest to your weight-on-the-back that they should resist sliding up and down the seat as you brake and accelerate. The best way to do this through the leg muscles rather than trying to hang on with the hands. Most motorcycle designers are sufficiently unthoughtful to provide the passenger with nothing

Introduce your passenger gently . . .

worthwhile to hold on to anyway. At all costs discourage them from hanging on around your waist since this will hinder your ability to control the motorcycle properly. With experience, passengers soon get the hang of using leg and back muscles to resist all but the fiercest acceleration or braking and learn to travel with hands resting on knees.

Previous page **Remember that passengers get frightened too**

Break passengers in gently to the idea of cornering. There is no point in rushing off to the nearest roundabout and proceeding to carve your way around in a shower of dragging footpeg sparks. It's one certain way to lose a friend—perhaps literally.

Make sure your passenger has found both footpegs and is comfortable inside what is probably an unfamiliar helmet before you move off. It is also worth organising a signalling system in the event that the passenger wants to stop. Which may be sooner than you think if you don't take it steady enough. Putting passengers at ease will make them better quicker than scaring the living daylights out of them.

Assuming the passenger is sorted out, give a thought to the bike underneath you. As we have briefly mentioned the performance of the handling will have changed with the extra weight on the back seat. The steering may feel a little less direct. In some circumstances, particularly while accelerating, the control precision developed through mastery of the reverse steering technique will be lost. Naturally enough, it is easier to pull heart-stopping

wheelies with passengers on the back. Make sure your passenger is ready and willing for such extremes or you might find him—or her—suddenly disappearing backwards.

Severe braking will usually find the passenger becoming very friendly indeed but the extra weight does reduce the risk of locking up the rear wheel. Initially, the front tyre may not grip as well as expected, so panic braking may provoke a slide easier than you might expect. Once the weight of the machine

. . . before speeding things up

A good passenger stays in line with the bike

transfers forward, however, normal full braking can be used.

With the extra weight compressing the rear suspension, ground clearance will be reduced. What is less obvious is that the damping and suspension characteristics will be changed since they were designed with the solo rider in mind. Most machines have a rear spring pre-tension adjustment and the manufacturers recommend using the highest setting when carrying passengers. This helps to limit the reduced ground clearance but only the most expensive machines will have damping adjustment to match the increased load. As a result, ride height and spring performance may be good but damping inadequate. Riding with passengers under such circumstances makes the bike wallow, particularly around corners. Such inadequacies vary from bike to bike so it is impossible to give specific rules on how to overcome the problems. With the complex and almost infinitely adjustable suspension rapidly becoming available on more and more modern machines there is no reason for the suspension to be inadequate in any circumstances.

Passenger's vision is obscured

Assuming there may be many riders who do not have such machinery, there are a few things to look out for when carrying a passenger. With the reduced ground clearance, cornering clearance is also affected. If you are used to indulging in a little solo peg-scraping you will in fact be quite sensitive to the corresponding lean angle just before the more solid parts of the motorcycle touch the road and lead to disaster. With a passenger this maximum angle is less. If you are following recommended practice you will be trying to move

His or her life in your hands

Brake gently when two-up

as quickly as possible from upright to maximum cornering attitude. With the unfamiliar extra weight of a passenger, you will find maximum lean a lot quicker at what will appear pretty tame lean angles. However, as you rush to maximum lean remember to make allowances or else you may find all safety margins used up and hard metal lifting the back wheel off the ground.

Depending on the machine take great care when approaching any sort of limits. With the change in suspension geometry, rigid bits of

bike may touch the ground before the usual footpeg progressive sensors.

With less springing and doubtful damping, leave wide safety margins when scratching with passengers. Encountering a bump while cornering will have more effect than usual— severely reducing cornering clearance. Sometimes such incidents will bring the hard bits onto the ground with a bump. Usually this is more dramatic than dangerous as the suspension recoil will save things and allow regained control. This is not something that can be relied on.

If you are used to moving weight around while riding, warn your passenger and remember that it may be difficult to shuffle about with someone behind you. Passengers should be told to sit still and let you get on with it. With the apparent lightening of the

They can learn to enjoy it as well

front end it is sometimes a good idea to ride closer to the tank than normal, moving your weight further forward to counteract the rearward bias.

Riding with a passenger is the only area of expertise which does not have a racing example to use. This is in effect a stern warning. If hardbitten roadracers the world over have never had the nerve to race two-up, then the risks must be considerable. This lack of racing experience will more likely be caused by fear from the passengers' point of view rather than the riders'.

Remember that before laughing at someone who says they are a frightened passenger.

10 Reading the road

Once the techniques of steering, braking and acceleration are mastered there still remains one area which will never be fully learned. Motorcycles are ridden in a moving, changing and particularly dangerous environment—on the public highway. All that rests between safe progress and a likely spell in a hospital bed is the rider's skill—not just in handling his machine but in reading the environment in front of him. Observing and predicting the movement or effects of hazards is essential to staying alive.

It has already been mentioned that with time most riders develop a 'sixth sense' which forewarns them of danger and invokes unease when risks are being taken. What any rider must do is not wait for this sense to arrive but actively to study his actions and make it happen. Once aware of this subtle blend of human fears and subconscious predictions, the rider must continue to foster it, integrate it with his day to day riding and develop it with imagination and skill from successive experiences. Learn from every road situation, predicting well in advance the likely outcome of a particular junction encounter and then comparing the actual traffic movement with what you predicted.

Back this up with a responsible approach to fellow road users and a good appreciation of the road surface and you should have reached a plateau of riding achievement that guarantees as much safety as is reasonable. Never believe you are in complete security. On a machine with such inherent and easily pro-voked instability as a motorcycle operating in an environment over which the rider has no control, you will never be in complete safety. Confident you must be that blame for any incident cannot be attached to you.

Slides on ice or a greasy surface are your own fault—you should have seen or predicted the danger. Likewise other road users can never be entirely to blame. You must expect them to behave completely irrationally, pulling out of junctions without looking and cutting across your path without considering your abilities to avoid them. Such incidents in theory place no blame on the threatened road user—you—but until such time as there is complete road sense understanding by everyone out there they will continue unabated. So you must expect complete disregard for your personal welfare from every other lunatic on the road. That's right, lunatic. For that is how you must treat them if you are to stay alive to ride another day.

There's no point in being nihilistic or attempting can't be bothered philosophy by saying, 'If it's going to happen, it will.' There is a responsibility on behalf of everyone who has the privilege of the highway to take as much care as possible—not just of their own safety but for the simple reason that in an accident, you cannot predict how many others will be involved.

Every incident of highway stupidity will make you question why, if they drive so comprehensively appallingly, you need to struggle to improve your own already high standards.

Anticipate hazards on the road surface

The question is inevitable but the temptation to ease off and relax a little must be resisted, falsely secure that you are better than the majority when the answer is so difficult. Live and ride not by the standards of the lowest examples but by the excellence which none of us have yet reached.

The right mental approach will depend on you as an individual. Many regard this kind of road safety as beneath their dignity not to mention their ego. Such people are convinced that they have the ability, above all others, to ride blindingly aggressively in every situation and get away with it. As the sad figures

Speed on a strange road can provide all kinds of excitement. Be prepared

for motorcycle accidents show, this is unlikely to be the case.

Reading the road can be split into two identifiable areas, the road surface and the traffic conditions.

Road surface reactions

Sliding along the road with a wrecked machine, fearful of impending broken bones, is no time to remember how vulnerable motorcycles are to the road surface beneath. Yet with all the other more obvious threats of lunatic drivers it is easy to forget that above

all other road-users a motorcycle's stability depends on the road beneath.

Riders who spend most of their time in a city environment are probably more aware than others of just how dangerous road surfaces can become with the build up of traffic grease mixed with a little water.

It is rain that poses the biggest threat to the two wheeler. Already we have said that wet roads should be treated with the greatest care and that any attempts at hurrying must be forgotten.

In torrential rain the tyres must work particularly hard to move the water before they can begin to provide the grip you need. Never forget just how much water lies on the road. Motorcycles, with their more round section than car tyres are less prone to aquaplaning. They are certainly not immune from it and worn tyres will be even more dangerous. Such heavy rain conditions as will be necessary to make a motorcycle aquaplane will be accompanied by such a drastic reduction of visibility that you would need to be pretty dumb to travel at anything like sufficient speed to start aquaplaning. Remember though, there's one born every minute. . . .

Roads are often poorly drained, with the result that when it is raining, water will flow across the road surface in its search for the lowest spot. These temporary rivers are quite visible and you should slow down before passing through them. Motorways often feature those special hazards, just where you expect fast progress to be at its safest. If possible, try to ride through them on a dry line left by vehicles travelling in front and gain full advantage of the work already done by their tyres. Do not travel too close behind simply to draw this marginal benefit. On a rainy night, with oncoming headlights dazzling and

Keep away from the grit at the road edge

reflecting off a wet road, such features are very hard to see—slow down to a safe speed.

Increasingly, diesel and other fuel oil is spilt from other vehicles, particularly around the outside of sharper corners. In cities, with their profusion of junctions and press-on traffic, the problem is at its worst. After prolonged dry periods there is a build up of oil, rubber and anything else slippery you can think of. A quick shower and this whole mess lifts off the road and with passing traffic is turned into a filthy emulsion with considerable lubricating qualities. Unsuspecting motorcyclists will find their posteriors in swift and sudden contact with the road. Diesel is often difficult to see in wet weather. If it has been spilled recently it will leave tell-tale oily marks spreading over the wet surface. These soon disappear with passing traffic as the diesel is whipped into the surface water. In especially busy areas, diesel build up in the dry is so large that when it does rain, water is repelled by the grease and sits in globules on the road. Definitely something to be avoided.

Oil and water do not mix and neither do motorcycles with such a combination. That's the only rule that applies. Except that you can fall off anywhere.

In the dry, the diesel threat remains but is generally more visible. Any darker patches on a dry road should be avoided but even if you do run over such a problem and begin to slide, there is always the relative safety of a dry, secure surface nearby on which to correct matters. When it is wet, diesel can be spread quite a distance from where it was originally poured, removing any kind of safe haven.

In the country the threat of diesel is lessened but replaced with other delights like mud, the leftover evidence of passing horses, perhaps, and blocked ditches flooding the road. Anticipate these problems and never travel so fast that avoiding action is impossible.

Finally, road authorities add to all these problems with metal manhole covers which polish smooth and when wet offer no grip whatsoever. Road markings often have similar grip qualities. These are less of a problem to the cautious rider with a reasonable safety margin. Either he can skirt round them by taking gentler avoiding tactics or even run over them since he can easily see the limit of any possible slide. Negotiate such hazards with a trailing throttle.

Back to dry conditions, there are a number of other hazards which can impair the expected performance of your machine. First of all, consider bumps. Imagine a small but vicious upward bump. When braking hard the bump is likely to provide a slide. Accelerate hard over it and the front wheel may come up and be pulled down suddenly as the rear wheel runs over it. Try cornering over such an obstacle and your bike will be displaced sideways a short distance with a bit of a weave thrown in depending on your bike. All this is quite good fun and fairly predictable stuff.

When the bump gets bigger and turns into a crest, something like a hump-backed bridge, the effects become more extreme. Braking hard over such an object can make the front wheel break away as you are just over the apex. Accelerating hard will lift the front wheel high in the air and if the rear wheel drops down the dip slope too vigorously may be enough to flip the bike over which is very dramatic but usually equally expensive. Cornering over this obstacle will run the risk of the rear end stepping out as the rise is crested and the power is being wound on.

Encountered at a steady speed, humps like this can launch man and machine into mid-air. How such things are dealt with will largely then be in the lap of the gods. In such instances, stand up and allow the machine to hop about underneath. Try to keep the bike as upright and well balanced as possible.

Different surfaces provide different amounts of grip. Basically there are two types of road surface in common use, asphalt and concrete. Asphalt is the most common type and varies considerably, depending on the kind of dressing it has of stone chips. Concrete is usually reserved for motorways and has good grip in the dry but often holds water when wet. Sometimes the approaches to junctions and pedestrian crossings will be covered with a particularly high grip and abrasive surface. Look out for such changing surfaces near traffic hazards and use the extra grip to full advantage.

The kind of resurfacing that involves spray-ing the road with tar and then liberally sprinkling with some stone chips is fine for a short time but often deteriorates very rapidly. Large patches of shiny tar are the result, often appearing after hot weather. When wet such patches closely resemble the grip characteristics of wet manholes and are much larger.

For one reason or another, roads seem to be a prime target for hole diggers. Once the hole is refilled, the repairs to the road surface can spell disaster for the biker. Awkward bumps in difficult positions, potholes and a particularly nasty phenomenon—sealing the

Don't get too close to the kerb

edge of a repair with a shiny bitumen line. When wet such lines are lethal.

Road surfaces must attract your attention and you should mentally catalogue each type and its characteristics in the wet or dry. When riding on unfamiliar surfaces, get used to them before taking any liberties.

In cold weather, ice and snow are obvious problems. If it is cold enough, never trust a dry road to be ice free. Dips in the road may hold water and have frozen over. Blocked ditches can have flooded a road locally and caused icing over. The possibilities are endless and must be looked out for.

Traffic conditioning
Apart from observing the road surface, other factors must be taken into account. Only by applying a sensible and tolerant attitude to

Roadworks in front of you. What will the bump do to the handling?

other road users will you become a reasonably safe rider. The vulnerability of the motor-cyclist should never be forgotten. Always ride defensively, ready to back down from danger of threatening behaviour from other road users. Aggressive riding, carving up others and imposing your will on the road conditions sooner or later ends up as a disaster.

We have covered the recommended atti-tude to motorcycling and included reference to anticipating hazards to be better prepared for them. Anticipation demands advance knowledge gained by looking as far ahead as possible to see forthcoming junctions, dangers in the road surface and likely traffic levels. Mastery of this ability, often referred to as 'roadcraft' separates the advanced rider from the crowd.

Although the need for constant observation and readiness is essential and obvious in a town environment, it is equally important though less apparent in a country environment. On today's congested roads you simply cannot relax an instant without running risks.

Before considering observation, think about the eyes. With increasing speed, the natural human reaction is to look further ahead. This is a good safety point but as you do so, nearby detail becomes less visible while it poses the greatest threat. When riding quickly, deliberately keep scanning your immediate environment as well as looking ahead.

Part of the attraction of bikes is their ability to pass traffic easier than any other vehicle. Since motorcycles are therefore overtaking more frequently than any other vehicle, then the high risk involved in passing manoeuvres is encountered all the more often, sometimes even constantly. It is easy to become too familiar with this situation and ignore the risks involved in overtaking. Couple this with the aforementioned effect of the eyes with increasing speed and the risk is that vehicles can pull out to turn right or overtake without your noticing them until it is too late.

Also on the overtaking front, at high speed your eyes will be looking as far ahead as possible. On a motorway, for instance, you may be overtaking slower traffic. Because of your speed, however, you cannot pay as much attention to traffic on your inside. Slow down in situations like this until your fellow travellers can be paid the fullest attention. It becomes apparent that the most danger provoking element in overtaking is not the actual speed but the differential speed between you and the slower vehicle. Tearing past typical motorway traffic at 120 mph will give you a speed differential of around 60 mph. Stand at the edge of a road six feet from traffic at 60 mph and the danger becomes very apparent.

The speed differential equation does not only apply at high speeds. In slow moving traffic, feeding down the outside should never be considered at more than walking pace. Some halfwit motorist is very likely to open his door to see what is happening or execute a U-turn without looking in the hope of finding another, quicker route. The danger of cruising past stationary traffic at 60 mph becomes obvious.

As a rough rule it is unwise to pass other vehicles at anything more than 15–20 mph faster than they are travelling, even if there is considerable distance between you.

When overtaking even parked vehicles look out for signs that they are about to pull out. Check parked cars for drivers. If there is someone inside, it will quite possibly pull out suddenly. Look for puffs of exhaust gases, indicating a car that may be being started.

Once things are moving, check cars before you pass them. If necessary make sure they have seen you moving up the outside by flashing a headlight or positioning yourself behind them for a while. Look out for cars that are about to overtake, even if they are not signalling. As we have said, cars overtake less frequently than motorcycles. Thus the driver is less confident than the motorcyclist and more likely to have attention completely absorbed by judging speed and distance rather than looking for additional hazards around him.

When overtaking larger vehicles, hang back until you are certain that you have the necessary power to overtake. Look also for signs of traffic ahead, pulling out in front of the vehicle you wish to overtake. Never take notice of someone's signal to wave you past an obstruction other than as an indication that they have seen you. When passing trucks or buses, watch out for crosswinds as you break through the aerodynamic wake of the vehicle. They can cause quite a wobble to even the largest of machines.

In heavy traffic, vehicles invariably travel too close together, often so close as to make it difficult to pull in after overtaking. Before starting to overtake, make sure there will be sufficient clear space for you to pull into when you get there.

Through good observation stay well prepared for junctions, even in strange and unfamiliar territory. Find the right traffic lane as early as possible and follow the road signs. Watch out too for pedestrians and cyclists. Both are prone to even more irrational and sudden behaviour than car drivers. You are likely to be passing them at more than the optimum 15–20 mph overtaking speed. In towns be prepared for pedestrians walking out from behind parked vehicles, particularly ones that you cannot see through.

At some time or other, you will be caught in a motorway or dual carriage way traffic jam. Remember that filtering in between two lanes of cars is twice as dangerous as filtering along the outside of one queue of cars. The larger the hold up the more likely it is that people will be opening doors to see what is happening or trying to change lane into a faster moving one.

By devious observation look for signs that may provoke irrational behaviour from motorists. A petrol station may suddenly seem like a good idea to the driver in front and he will make a beeline for it without thinking of signalling. Schools are likely to have kids around them totally absorbed in football or beating each other up and not road safety. Factory gates may suddenly turn into human flood gates as knocking off time arrives.

There are many, many more examples to look for. All your predictions may not prove accurate but at least you will have been ready to meet them. If it has not been said enough already, fellow road users and your own poor judgement are the biggest hazards on the road. So watch out.

11 Be prepared

The appeal of the motorcycle is its immediacy. Throw a leg over a bike and it is instant excitement. Unfortunately all this euphoric, action-packed stuff is not quite the reality. The weather interferes. Cold, wet and even the heat can make long trips more of a test of human endurance than prolonged pleasurable entertainment. For a quick trip down the road or the journey to work you can get away with limited protective clothing. Not just protection from bumps and scrapes but from the elements as well.

On a longer trip careful attention to detail helps the trip enormously, easing the physical comfort of rider and his passenger if he has one, and helping the trip run more smoothly by careful route preparation.

The first and essential piece of riding equipment is a helmet. Broadly there are two types available—full face and open face and most will know the difference. As an all round and all weather choice, the full enclosure helmet is the best, providing good face protection. When buying a helmet it is best not to be too determined to have a particular style before you have tried it on. It seems that while every manufacturer naturally offers a range of sizes, they all have a different idea of what shape the average human head is. Some helmets nip the temples, others squeeze your ears. It is essential that you find a helmet with a firm, all round comfortable fit or else long trips will be agony. A helmet that feels even a little tight when worn for the first time will feel like an ever-tightening vice after a few hours. Check that there are no tight spots before you buy it. Just because new helmets are nice and soft inside, shiny outside and the salesman will not stop talking don't be rushed into buying something less than a perfect fit. Wander about the showroom for ten minutes if necessary.

There must be some safety advantage in searching out a well fitting, comfortable helmet but more important is your own comfort. It's you who has to wear it. On the whole, it is good advice to buy as good a helmet as you can afford but be warned that a large price is not necessarily indicative of a large degree of safety.

Visors are the one drawback on a full face helmet. They all scratch after a while, making good vision difficult in dark or wet conditions. Replace visors as often as they need it. On more modern helmets visors are making a better and better seal against draughts. Sometimes a helmet will have an annoying draught across, say, the eyes making them water to the point of interfering with good sight. On long trips this will become a real pain. Unfortunately you cannot road test helmets before buying so you may end up lumbered with an unsatisfactory one.

If there are any annoying draughts on a new helmet, take care if you try to seal them up. In some fairly rarified instances, wrapping scarves around the neck and then stuffing them up under the helmet to keep out the wind has led to the motorcyclist losing control through a lack of oxygen. Obviously you cannot cut off all your air supply.

With open face helmets the same principles of fit and comfort apply. If you are considering doing any sort of speed an open face with a peak will be very tiring on the neck muscles and will require goggles and possibly a scarf. In cold weather it is recommended to use at least a scarf wrapped over the nose if you cannot afford a full face helmet. At anything above inner city speeds make sure you have some eye protection. Rain with an open face helmet and unprotected face will be a painful experience.

There is not a great deal to be said about gloves except that you should wear warm ones in the winter and swap to thinner leather ones in the summer. Waterproofing gloves seems to remain impossible although rubber household gloves, however inelegant, pulled over the top of your riding gloves are the only certain method of waterproofing the hands so far discovered. Waterproof mittens do work better but they limit action of the controls and leak eventually. In winter the best way of keeping fingers warm is with a good pair of real sheepskin mittens covered with waterproof overmitts. In all conditions except the warmest heated handlebar grips can provide amazingly welcome warmth for the hands. They may sound a bit of a pansy accessory but they do ward off those cold, stiffened fingers.

After the helmet and gloves, boots are the next consideration. It is a bit impractical to change into them for every journey you ever make but on long trips they make life a good deal more comfortable. In the wet, wellingtons or the excellent designed-for-the-job motorcycle rubber boots are the only way to stay dry. Well polished leather boots will keep out the rain for a couple of hours but will eventually begin to leak. For general work a good pair of shoes or boots will do the job admirably with a pair of stretchy rubber overshoes. In terms of physical protection, however, the only choice is leather boots. Somehow or other the feet always seem to come out of tumbles quite badly so don't dismiss leather boots without giving them careful consideration. Good ones are certainly the most comfortable kind of footwear around.

Waterproof clothing is an area in which the combined weight of modern technology does not yet seem to have improved matters although many are close. In the end, however, they all seem to leak. Wherever you ride, some form of waterproof clothing will be necessary. There are two choices: lightweight, single layer waterproof fabric; or the heavier fully lined type, sometimes with a foil interlining to keep the warmth in. The former is naturally the least expensive and is pretty versatile. It can be used in any temperature and is usually large enough to allow you to build up a few layers of clothing beneath to combat the intense cold. The heavier alternatives are excellent for the task they were designed for—long distance, serious riding in all weathers. If they do begin to leak and the lining gets a soaking they can be difficult to dry out if they are needed the next day. Most riders will know which kind of clothing will suit them best but will probably be left making do with what they can afford.

Warmth and practicality should be bought above all else. One day designers may wake up and at least try to make it all look a bit more socially acceptable but until then it's best to leave your vanity behind and stay warm and dry. I have already mentioned the dangers of cold fingers fumbling for delicate controls. The same applies to the rest of your body. There is no enjoyment in getting

An open face alternative to the full enclosure helmet. Two piece riding suit completes the outfit

Leathers and full face helmet are the uniform . . .

freezing cold. It takes all the fun out of motor-cycling. Comfort and correct dress will help you to enjoy your motorcycling that much more.

Often held to be the ultimate in riding gear is leather clothing. It certainly is best in terms of abrasion resistance if a good, tough leather is used. Primarily, choose a good cowhide but there are other types which provide equally good protection. In particular, avoid anything made from sheep's leather which offers little more protection than a pair of jeans. Good hide on the other hand can sometimes go through tumbles and slides without marking at all.

Leather clothing looks by far the best but offers little in the way of warmth. Its draught beating qualities are good and the one thing most striking about wearing leathers is the lack of flapping that goes on. Only when you have worn leathers on a long trip do you realise how tiring a flapping rain suit can be.

When pulling on all this gear put gloves over the outside of the suit sleeves. When cruising in the rain, water will then flow up onto the suit rather than up the inside. For the same reasons it is best to wear any over-suit over the top of boots to keep the water running off the suit on the outside. Wearing boots over the outside of a suit will encourage water to flow down inside them.

When wearing any clothing and particularly leathers the aim is to make sure that whatever happens if you fall off no bare flesh is left exposed.

Comfort in all weathers will depend on your machine. Some bikes have adjustable handle-

Next page; Left . . . **for the men who mean business**

Next page; Right **Jacket and jeans alternative**

bars and footpegs. It's worth experimenting to find the position that makes you the most comfortable for all types of riding. Don't simply set them at the position that you think looks the most racy. It is bound to feel unnatural. For road riding there can be additional dangers to a radical seating position. Bending arms and legs tightly to be able to hold onto the controls can restrict the blood supply, shortening the time it takes to get cold.

Long trips will probably involve travelling by unfamiliar routes. Map reading is difficult on a motorbike so it is worthwhile planning the route in advance. Write down the successive road numbers that you intend to follow noting where the junctions are and stick this on the top of the tank. It should reduce the number of stops to look at the map to a minimum. Again, preparation pays dividends in terms of time saved and peace of mind.

Luggage will also play a part in your comfort. Two kinds are available, hard and soft. Hard luggage usually takes the form of a top box or panniers. Of the two, panniers are better general purpose luggage. The top box is only suitable for very light items since it is not advisable to place any weight so high up and far back. Doing so could inspire some pretty amazing high speed wobbles. Panniers give a better weight distribution and can thus be loaded far heavier but are unfortunately more expensive.

If you take the soft luggage option, which is more easily removed if you don't want to spoil the looks of your bike, go for a tank bag first followed by throw-over panniers. Tank bags put luggage weight in the best possible position and offer some chest protection into the bargain. Some of the larger ones can restrict the steering lock or your view of the instruments so be ready for such shortcomings. Throw-over panniers can provide useful extra carrying capacity but can also hinder a passenger's comfort. Most hard luggage is completely waterproof but with soft luggage it is best to prewrap everything in plastic bags. At the end of a long, wet trip nothing is worse than finding your change of clothing is soaked as well.

Boring though it may be preparation is the only way to get serious riding done in comfort.

12 Here's looking at you . . .

It's pretty well established that a motorcyclist is one of an enthusiast breed. Someone who is steeped in the whole scene; has friends who share his excitement of two wheels; and would not travel any other way.

Such dedication is unlikely to be satisfied simply by riding to work each day. Motorcycles will be talked about, thought about and looked at, examined. Such examination builds up a knowledge of current and past machinery, charting the development of the motorcycle. That development is taking place at increasing pace. Already a whirlwind of new models whisks past the consumer's eye only to be replaced by more exotic, flash or ostentatious examples of two wheel design a year later.

Through all this fashionable flash most of us make do with a new bike only occasionally. For all the development we still search for individuality, adapting vehicles for our own self-expression rather than rustling along with the crowd on identical bikes.

To join in the traditional treadmill of biking we need to develop a coherent approach to assessing the qualities of new or strange machinery without merely being wooed by manufacturers' superlatives. Through all the advertising and promotion the consumer needs to stand back, look long and hard at the motorcycle in front of him and then draw his own conclusions based on his own needs.

Searching for such decisions is difficult with today's machinery. Technology flashing past our very eyes can confuse and blind you to the real purpose of motorcycling. Complex, multi-cylindered, myriad valved wonders almost defy description let alone provoke serious, cool-minded assessment. To extract the most from your bike demands a knowledge and understanding of its function.

A rider needs to build a rapport with the machine and this can be done all the quicker if he understands what the designer tried to achieve. For beneath all the flash and glitter motorcycles are particularly functional pieces. Every single part is there for a reason. Once you appreciate that reason the better you will understand your motorcycle.

You should look at bikes before riding them and try to predict their likely behaviour, not from the stylist's whim with colour and aggressive stickers but from the motorcycle that lies beneath. Once riding, concentrate on the bike's success as a machine and not as an extension to the ego. Does the suspension work? Is the power adequate? Does the whole thing wobble, snake or scare you to death? Are the tyres up to their job?

Every week and every month specialist motorcycle newspapers and magazines go through this process with varying degrees of professionalism. It is, however, difficult for them to act as judges on your behalf. Only you will know exactly which bike or set of riding qualities suit you best. So the task is to be sufficiently independent of mind to know what you want and not to be led by the over the top claims of vested interests. Listen, but don't necessarily believe it.

Big machines usually have big power. Bags of horsepower is seductive and certainly has a place in motorcycling. Unfortunately, it is also associated with bulk and excessive weight which make some equally heavy demands of the handling and steering. Big bikes will always be with us because there is nothing to beat the feeling of muscle as their huge torque surges you forward from 100 mph. As yet, smaller bikes cannot equal such performance.

Smaller machines can still provide equivalent levels of excitement. They are lighter in

Put faith in your machine when you understand it

weight, usually steer better and are more agile.

Once you have chosen the type of machine that suits you best, get to know it. Feel for its suspension and understand it power characteristics. Get to know its limitations and advantages. If you are good at this process of mechanical appreciation, when it comes to personalising your motorcycle you will stand more chance of making changes for the better

Adjusting rear suspension

Anti-dive systems are designed to help front suspension under braking

in the important areas of suspension, brakes and performance.

If you have been misled and don't really understand the machine, any changes you make may be largely cosmetic or even detrimental to the original objective which must have been to improve performance.

Apart from tailoring your bike to your own particular needs never forget that without good maintenance real enjoyment will elude you. There is no point in taking risks on an old nail stuck together with strips of tinplate and odd sized nuts and bolts, worried by the thought of it all collapsing underneath you.

However old the bike is there is no excuse for worn out bearings, ineffective brakes or bald tyres. Part of appreciating a machine is being prepared to look after it and complete essential maintenance. It's far nicer to ride with a decent chain, well oiled control cables and tyres with tread. Instead of waiting for something to fail, enjoy the ride.

Be prepared to accept mechanical limitations as well. Older machines—and perhaps some modern ones—can be prone to difficulties if they are maltreated or overworked. Clutches, brakes and shock absorbers can all fade and rapidly lose efficiency. Give them a

Opposite; Above **High bars sit you upright**

Left **Well-maintained machinery helps**

Above **Experiment with balance on a new machine**

chance to cool and things will start to work again properly but do not press on with failing equipment.

Remember too that any machine goes through considerable change even under normal conditions. The wheelbase, for instance, gets shorter as you brake. The whole machine gets lighter as you use fuel. Handling may change as the tyres wear down their profile. Be sensitive to these changing factors which may explain gradual changes to the performance of your machine.

Look at the overall dimensions of a machine before riding it. The longer the wheelbase the more sluggish the machine will be to turn into corners. A steep fork angle will to some extent counteract this but may make instabilities associated with high speed set in at quite a slow pace.

There are many other phenomena attached to the mysterious science of motorcycle handling. Half the challenge of riding a motorcycle is learning to appreciate the mechanical inexactitude, the jumble of compromise that makes up today's machine. The other half is being capable, in spite of everything, to ride motorcycles effectively—right up to their limits without taking unnecessary risks.

13 Where to now?

Through the pages of this book I have so far looked at the process of riding and increasing ability from what I hope is a new and positive standpoint. Now we must consider the status of motorcycling and how it is likely to develop.

Motorcycling has been too apologetic for its existence in the face of strident safety campaigning from people who will never appreciate the spirited freedom it offers. It is, I feel, time for motorcycling to reassert itself from the grassroots—each and every rider must think about their part in the spreading and complex jigsaw of the motorcycling image.

You cannot deny that motorcycling is dangerous compared to other less exciting forms of transport. In earlier chapters I have discussed why this is so, why the risks are receding too slowly to quieten our critics. Now we must consider how, as individual motorcyclists, we can make the massive jump in standards required—not just to placate the misguided legislators but to establish a new set of values to ensure motorcycling continues to provide the same rushing excitement we so value.

Rebellion is a quality much talked about when considering motorcycling. What we need now is rebellion. Not a misguided show of ugly, brutish hordes demanding action but a quiet rebellion on behalf of every rider to seek expression through their riding. Each one of us must raise our own standards. If we succeed with a balanced and considered approach then a better safety record will be a welcome side effect. Many are obviously following such a code of passive rebellion—keep it going but don't be pompous about it.

I hope to have set out a few guidelines in the preceding chapters which will go some way to break down the prevailing situation. It will remain up to individuals to pull all the strands of ideas and techniques from the text. What is written is, I believe, as close as one can get to defining the action of riding a motorcycle. Undoubtedly, if the themes mentioned are taken up and used by every rider to improve his skills then we will have begun a new dialogue with the motorcycle. Maybe we will achieve a significant reduction in the accident rate without the need to kill off the very reason we all enjoy motorcycling.

Although I have attempted to explain the riding process in some depth, given time and experiment by everyone new ideas and theories will help to inspire and develop a constantly improving approach. With luck and acceptance I hope this book will be a beginning rather than be expected to hold all the answers.

Every rider must develop their own ideas based on the essentials of machine handling. Those who design machines may attempt to achieve particular handling characteristics but they will never be able to account for individual riders' different habits and techniques.

To sum up the approach necessary to get the most from this book; always stay prepared to learn. Try to accelerate the learning process through experimentation but always recognise your limits and don't exceed them.

Opposite ; Above **Blending all techniques together**   *Above* **Express yourself through riding**

Left **Never stop learning**

The camaraderie of motorcycling will be put to the test in future years as burgeoning legislation emasculates the thrill of motorcycling. To individual motorcyclists, their favourite activity can be many things. It can be exciting, relaxing or just plain good fun. But to some in authority it is simply an excessively dangerous activity which has no place in a civilized society. They will not be persuaded otherwise unless motorcycling can show itself worthy of its existence.

What we do not need is the forever defensive tactics so far displayed by many of motorcycling's responses to legislation. Training schemes and propaganda have never seriously addressed the root of the problem. They go some way towards improving motorcycling standards but are flawed by not giving sufficient thought to the motivation of the people they train. Industry response to legislation in its earliest stages and during implementation is a short sighted shambles. Motorcycling's activist groups do nothing to help an already poor image.

We must make the quiet rebellion in the only way we can—by improving our riding. Don't forget that motorcycling must remain what it really is—skilfully controlled excitement.

Left **Is there a way forward for motorcycling?**